Staying in Tune

Staying in Tune

From American Idol to Nashville,
how the Young Women values have
helped me remain true to the gospel

CARMEN RASMUSEN

spring creek
BOOK COMPANY
Provo, Utah

ISBN 13: 978-1-932898-89-7

e. 1

Published by:
Spring Creek Book Company
P.O. Box 50355
Provo, Utah 84605-0355

www.springcreekbooks.com

Cover design © Spring Creek Book Company
Cover photo credit: Jason Olsen, Deseret Morning News
Cover photo © Deseret Morning News
Back cover photos and interior photos courtesy of Carmen Rasmusen.
Used by permission.

Printed in the United States of America
10 9 8 7 6 5 4 3 2 1
Printed on acid-free paper

Library of Congress Control Number: 2007940191

Dedication

To my family,
for helping me stay "in tune!"

Acknowledgments

Thank you Brad for always believing in me, for all the late night, last-minute editing sessions, and for taking over the dishes and the laundry while I sat on the couch writing.

Thank you to everyone at Spring Creek Books who helped put this thing together so quickly—especially Chad and Tammy Daybell for their support and for taking a chance with a first-time writer.

Thank you to all my family members who gave me wonderful advice and suggestions when I needed them, especially Dad, Mom, Camille, Jeanette, Gary and Kim. I feel truly blessed to have you all in my life.

TABLE OF CONTENTS

A Note from Carmen

Throughout this book there are specific stories from my life that relate to the seven Young Women values—Faith, Divine Nature, Individual Worth, Knowledge, Choice and Accountability, Good Works, and Integrity.

The value experiences are in no particular order, however they each collaborate with a certain time in my life.

Even though I've since graduated from the Young Women program, I've still relied on the important lessons I've learned from striving to live each value and hold them all close to my heart.

INTRODUCTION

Not Britney

"Keep your body covered and no decent man will ever think less of you for it, and every good, honorable man who would think of marrying you would love you more for it."

—President Spencer W. Kimball

"I have this vision of you looking like Britney Spears."
My mouth fell open.

"Um . . . I'm sorry," I began, glancing nervously at my mom, "but I can't wear that."

That referring to a tiny pink halter top and white mini-skirt the famous stylist from *People* magazine was "visualizing" about.

"Excuse me?" he asked incredulously.

"I'm a good little Mormon girl!" I said with a laugh, hoping he'd catch on. Instead, he just looked at me like I was crazy.

"I'll be right back." He stormed out of the room.

Oh, boy. Sure I loved to sing. And dance. Yes, I had blonde hair, but that's pretty much all Britney Spears and I had in common! I was now a finalist on *American Idol* and I was looking forward to doing this photo shoot for *People*, but my excitement was quickly dashed when I saw my outfit—or lack of it. As the stylist walked out of the room, my mom took my hand and pulled me down on the couch next to her. "What am I going to do?" I asked desperately.

She looked past me and whispered, "Carmen, look at how cute that shirt is!"

I turned around to see where she was pointing, and hanging in a closet across the hall was a sparkly red button-down shirt. It was *gorgeous*. But what was I going to do? Just grab a random shirt and tell the most popular fashion guru in the business that I was more qualified to choose my wardrobe?

"You're right," I said, "but I don't know whose shirt it is. I can't wear that! Even if I could, what would go with it?"

"The jeans you have on look good." She smiled encouragingly. "Go ask him!"

The stylist soon reappeared, poking his head in the room. "Carmen? Can I talk to you for a second?" He impatiently grabbed my hand and pulled me out of the room, shutting the door firmly behind us, leaving my mom on the couch. I guess he wanted to get me away from her, thinking that she was the one influencing my decision not to wear the skimpy outfit.

In a way, he was right. But what he didn't know was that before I came out to Los Angeles, I had made a very important promise on my own—a promise that needed to be made on my knees. This was a promise I was *determined* to keep.

"Now, listen," the stylist began. "I hand-picked this outfit specifically for you. I want you in PINK and WHITE, okay? Do you know who I am? Trust me, this will look good."

I glanced once more at the red shirt hanging in the closet behind us. Biting my lip, I took a chance.

"Can I just wear that?" I asked desperately, pointing to the top. He turned to look at it as I quickly rushed on, "I know it's not what you pictured, but I *promise* I can make it look just as good as what you were hoping for. Better, even! Let me try it on for you."

"That's a five hundred dollar shirt," he said. "I don't know whose it is. It was probably left over from another shoot."

"*Please*, let me try it on. If you don't like it, we'll think of something else." Not having a clue what "something else" would be, I snatched the shirt from the hanger and ran into the dressing room before he could change his mind.

Please, please let this fit, I prayed as I slipped the shirt over my shoulders. Amazing—not only was it my size, it actually went perfectly with my jeans. I knew even before I walked out that I was going to get to wear it. Feeling confident, I opened the door to show the stylist *my* vision. One look is all he took. One look, up and down.

"Yes," he said. "Okay. That will work. Let's do it."

After a quick visit to the hair and make-up room, we were led through the lush hotel to a Mustang convertible parked outside. There were lights shining on the beautiful white car, and as I walked out, people on the street stopped to watch as I climbed into the car and began to pose for the camera.

I felt like a movie star. It felt so glamorous! But more importantly, I had kept my promise to Heavenly Father to dress modestly. I knew it wasn't a coincidence that I found that red shirt.

Two weeks later, fellow contestant Clay Aiken came up to me to show me the latest issue of *People*. "It looks like someone sure liked you, Miss Centerfold," he said with a smile.

"What do you mean?"

"Look, you've got the only two-page spread!"

I took the magazine from him to see what he was talking

about. I slowly began to flip through the pages. Each *American Idol* finalist looked *so* beautiful. Everyone had a photo spread across a full page, along with a little blurb about their likes and dislikes off to one side.

Everyone, that is, except me. Clay was right. My picture was the only one spread across two pages. I guess even the editors at *People* noticed how attractive modesty can be!

CHAPTER ONE

A Little Bit Country

"You sound like a cowgirl!"
—A compliment from my friend Dana
Jones, fourth grade, after I got done
singing in the bathroom at recess

From the time I could talk, I've loved to sing. We have silly home videos of my older sister Camille and I entertaining the family singing together while my younger brother Robby and little sister Raquel, did cartwheels in front of us.

We would have to occasionally let one of them sing "Blewty and the Beeeeast" or "I Love Basketball" but other than that, it was Camille and I who took center stage. (I would always roll my eyes when one of the little ones would get up to do an interesting version of their favorite song, when in reality, my buck-toothed impression of Shania Twain couldn't have been much better!)

My mom would frequently turn on Country Music Television (CMT) while she worked out on the treadmill downstairs, blasting the music through the entire house. I suppose that's how country became our music of choice. We would memorize the songs and try to mimic the singers. I got to where I could imitate Mindy McCready pretty darn well. My sister could do a mean Martina McBride, and we even learned how to harmonize together. (I was always the melody, because I had a hard time picking out the different parts.)

One of our favorite treats was going down to the music store and getting a new karaoke tape to perform along with. We actually started sounding pretty good, and my mom signed us up for every ward talent night, county fair, and singing group, and we auditioned for several plays. Performing wasn't something our parents pushed us into doing; we sincerely loved it, and we constantly had their support.

Many nights after dinner (especially if company was over) my mom would "encourage" Camille and I to sing a "little something." We'd always take too long to get ready. In fact, some nights it would take us close to an hour to work up the courage to perform. Finally, we'd come walking out, ready to put on one heck of a show but by then, our audience would have dwindled to just our mom and dad. We'd take one look at our poor turnout, and run bawling back to our rooms.

Our parents weren't very musical, but enjoyed listening to music. They would rent us old musicals such as *The Sound of Music* and *Meet Me in St. Louis*. One time, my mom even surprised Camille and I with our very own pair of pantaloons that she sewed herself—inspired by the girls in *Seven Brides for Seven Brothers*!

The very first memory I have of performing was at our little condo in Irvine, California. I was about 3 years old, and I loved listening to Radio Disney. Every time "Puff the Magic Dragon" would come on the radio, I'd run into my room and yell for my mom to get down my pink ballet outfit. I'd quickly set up all my teddy bears and dollies, put on my tutu, and then with my best "performing face" on (soft smile, close-lipped, eyes crinkled) I would dance for them. My mom admits that she doesn't even remember doing this, but it just goes to show how supportive and helpful she was when it came to doing things that I loved.

Back then, if I didn't know how to do something, I'd just fake it. I was really good at imitating other people. I guess that's what first convinced my parents of my singing abilities.

One day as my mom and I were driving in the car, I put in one of my favorite tapes: Paula Abdul. I began to sing along with the songs, mimicking her voice.

"You sound just like her!" my mom gushed. (Little did we know that several years later, I'd not only *meet* Paula Abdul, but that she would actually be judging my singing!)

I got away with sounding like other people for awhile (Paula Abdul, LeAnn Rimes, Shania Twain), but it wasn't until much, much later that I learned how to develop a unique style of my own.

♪ ♪ ♪
Choice and Accountability

My elementary school years were some of the best of my life. I loved school! I loved learning, I loved my teachers, I loved the little desks and pencil boxes. I loved the smell when you first walked into the school, and the squeaky sound my sneakers made on the gym floor. I especially loved eating "hot lunch" and the little cartons of chocolate and root beer milk.

One day while we were eating in the cafeteria, a boy named Jonathan started talking about his karate class. He was explaining what the different colors of belts stood for. It sounded so exciting, and for some reason I blurted out, "I'm in karate, too!"

"Yeah, right!" He burst out laughing, along with everyone else at the table.

"I am!" I protested, my face turning bright red.

"Okay," Jonathan said. "Then what color belt do you have?" *Color?* Um . . .

"I'm a green belt!" I announced. *Was green even one of the belt colors?*

"Cool!" he exclaimed. "That's pretty good!"

"Yeah . . ." Suddenly he was asking me all these questions and everyone was so interested and amazed that *I* knew *karate*, and it wasn't too long before I realized I had dug myself into a very deep hole.

When I got home from school, I told my mom what I had done. I don't remember much, but I do remember feeling guilty enough to know I had to set things right and tell the truth. I asked Camille what I should do, and she said I should tell everyone the truth at recess. I closed my eyes and imagined calling everyone over to our favorite old tree up on the hill, telling them I had lied about karate, and then quickly running away so they couldn't make fun of me.

The next day, I was sooo nervous. I had a *ton* of butterflies in my stomach by the time recess finally rolled around. Finally, right before the final bell rang, I gathered everyone together.

"Guys, I have to tell you something." Suddenly, a half circle formed around me and everyone just stood there, waiting and staring. It almost seemed as if they were expecting me to come clean. I took a deep breath.

"I-I'm not really in karate." I confessed. *Whew! That wasn't so b—*

"LIAR!" A boy suddenly shouted, making me jump. All of a sudden, in my 10-year-old mind, the circle seemed to be getting tighter and tighter and everyone began screaming louder and louder, pointing and laughing at me.

There was nowhere to escape. I suddenly felt like I was in a whirlpool spinning downwards, faster and faster into the hole I had dug for myself. I was sure that everyone would hate me forever for lying. But in actuality, by the time computer class rolled around, everyone had pretty much forgotten all about it. When I got home, my mom was waiting for me. She pulled me down on our couch next to her and handed me a little box. "Open it," she said.

Inside was a beautiful glass angel, standing underneath a heart-shaped wreath with flowers all around it. Everything was white except for the pink and blue flowers.

"When we choose to do what's right and ask for forgiveness when we do something wrong, we become just like this pretty white angel," she said. "This is for you, for doing something difficult that you knew was right, and to remind you to always try to stay pure and clean."

I loved that angel. I learned a very important lesson that day, and that angel stayed in my room for a long, long time.

CHAPTER TWO

Beehives and a Technicolor Coat

"Today in English, Brady Brown shot spit wads at me and one of them landed in my hair!"
—My April 15, 1999 journal entry at age 14

I think it goes without saying that our junior high years are some of the most awkward of our lives. Some of us make it through okay—others aren't quite so lucky. It's a time for major change, major decisions, and major drama!

On the last day of sixth grade, a guy friend of mine wrote "See you in junior high—it's gonna be bad!" in my yearbook. He was right!

I still vividly remember my very first day as a "sevie" at Mueller Park Junior High. I wore a big white shirt with "Gap" written across the front in red, jeans, and Doc Martins. I did my hair down and put a headband in—one of those white, stretchy kinds. Science was my first class, and *b-o-r-i-n-g*! Instead of taking notes, my friend and I counted how many times the teacher said "type thing" during the lecture.

6

The first year of junior high actually wasn't too bad—but that's probably because I missed more than half of it. This was the year I tried out to be in the Children's Chorus in the Broadway musical *Joseph and the Amazing Technicolor Dreamcoat* starring Donny Osmond—and made it! So while my classmates were busy adjusting to the seven-classes-a-day schedule, doing their homework and studying for tests, I was busy learning songs and dances, and memorizing stage positions.

I had never had so much fun in my life. Being in a play was the best of all worlds—you got to sing, dance and act! Because there were so many kids in the play, they split us into two children's choirs—the Bakers and the Butlers. I was in the Baker choir, and we were chosen to perform on *opening night* up at Kingsbury Hall in Salt Lake. I will never forget the feeling of being onstage and seeing Donny Osmond come out for the first time. The crowd went wild!

I felt like it was up to me personally to entertain the audience, and I thrived off of the attention. Because we performed in the wintertime, a lot of kids ended up getting sick and had to stay home. But out of the 30-plus shows we did, I never missed a single one.

We did some silly things before the shows, such as powdering the inside of our shoes to keep them from smelling. We were also asked to take a nap before each show. I would lay out my little sleeping bag on the floor among all my friends and try *so hard* to relax—but I was always too excited for the show to begin!

Somewhere in the middle of all the practices, homework, and rehearsals, I got braces on my teeth. I remember that day perfectly. I decided to get blue and green rubber bands on them, and it just so happened that I had them put on the night of a show. There was a part during Act I where Donny came over to us and shook our hands onstage. As he came over to me,

I whispered excitedly, "Donny, look! I got braces!" Either he'd never had them himself or had somehow forgotten how painful they were, because he reached out, grabbed my face and shook it back and forth saying, "Oh, they look so cute!" I wanted to kill him. My face was throbbing and I spent the next two songs trying inconspicuously to remove the metal from the inside of my cheeks.

This was also the time when I entered the Young Women's organization. I absolutely loved it! I remember pulling up to my first activity with my dad, and hearing a knock on the car window. I rolled it down, and right then and there I was asked if I would be interested in becoming the Beehive 2nd Counselor.

We had a HUGE Beehive class, up to fifteen girls at one point! I had a special bond with those girls that I didn't have with my school friends. It was here in Young Women's that I began to gain my own testimony of the gospel. There was no denying the sweet spirit that was always present in our classes. Because of the support I had in Young Women's I was able to make it through the next couple of years.

Up to that point in my life, I never really had any trouble with friends. I got along with everyone, and loved getting to know new people. But there were several girls in *Joseph* with me who, out of the blue it seemed, began acting . . . weird. I don't know why it happened, but all of a sudden I started having trouble with these few girls. They would leave me out, gossip behind my back, make plans without me, and generally make me feel bad about myself.

Of course, my mom said they were just jealous, but I wasn't really sure what the reason was. One time we were in a store together, and one of them used the classic phrase, "Carmen, look over there!" I looked, and in a split second, they were gone. I caught a glimpse of one of them trying to hide behind one of the clothes racks. I couldn't believe that they were trying to ditch me! It was an awful feeling, to know that I wasn't wanted in their little "group." Unfortunately, this wasn't the only time I've been left out.

Have you ever experienced the empty feeling of being left out or the joy of being included as "one of the group?" It's so important to reach out to those who are lonely! I know from personal experience how hard it is to be excluded.

I think girls are more prone to do stuff like that than guys are, but we need to rise above that stereotype! It doesn't just end with junior high, either. We have a responsibility to "comfort those that stand in need of comfort" (Mosiah 18:9) all our lives. I always try to remember that no one is better than anyone else.

The next time you see someone sitting alone, remember that he or she is a child of God and is deeply loved. Include them. Talk to them. Trust me, it doesn't have to be anything big, even a smile and a "hi" as you walk down the hall can do wonders for a person's self esteem. It did for me.

CHAPTER THREE

Student Body Disaster

"I'm so sick of this popular, non-popular stuff. I hate it. I wish there were no such thing, because I feel so left out. Next year, I wanna become good friends with everyone."

—My July 28, 1999 journal entry

In eighth grade, I tried out for cheer and made the team. I loved cheering at the games, and sometimes during practices, the other girls would spread out on the mats and ask me to sing "Blue" for them. But eventually I got sick of having to go to every game (and I wasn't too crazy about wearing those itchy uniforms). So, I decided to run for Student Body Office in ninth grade.

For my slogan, I decided to use a play on the movie title *Never Been Kissed* and used the campaign slogan "Never Been SBO." I even posed like Drew Barrymore on the DVD cover for some of my posters. Unfortunately, my hair was really, really short at the time and I had super-pale, broken-out skin, and people who saw the poster probably immediately thought of the movie and suddenly understood why I had never been kissed, either!

For my skit, I sang "You Win My Love" by Shania Twain, but I changed the words to "I Wanna Win Your Vote." I felt really confident about my chances after my skit, and as I walked past a classroom a boy that I knew shouted, "Carmen! I voted for you!" I smiled. *This is it,* I thought. *I'm really gonna make it!*

Later that afternoon, as I sat in the foyer waiting for the results, I thought about the other candidates. My biggest competitors were Aaron Neuenshwander, Klarissa Bahr, and Hailey Hodgkinsen. The names of the winners were to be read in alphabetical order, and I knew if Klarissa and Hailey's names were read first, I wouldn't stand a chance against Aaron.

Finally, we were called to the front foyer to hear the results. One of the Student Body advisors held up a sheet of paper and began to read the names.

"The new officers for the 1999-2000 school year are: Klarissa Bahr, Hailey Hodgkinsen . . . and Aaron Neuenshwander." My heart dropped to the floor. I was *devastated.* I hadn't tried out for cheer because I wanted to run for SBO, and now I wasn't going to be in anything. I felt unhappy, unlucky, and unpopular.

What was worse, as we were taking down posters in the cafeteria, all of a sudden my friend Kiera let out a weird sound that sounded like something between a laugh and a gasp.

"What?" I asked, and walked over to where she was standing. Hesitantly, she handed me the poster with my picture on it, the one of me posing like Drew Barrymore . . . now sporting a mustache.

Up until then, I hadn't really let my emotions show, but after I saw the poster, I broke down into tears.

I can look back on that whole experience now and laugh but

it was really painful at the time, as shown by my journal entry the day after the election:

April 17, 1999

Sorry I didn't write yesterday. Feelings were too strong, I guess. No, I didn't make SBO. Klarissa, Aaron, and Hailey did. I did my skit but it was . . . okay. Then, I had to wait all day to find out. Amanda told me for sure I would make it, because they had to check all the ballots and every one had my name on them. Oh, well. Maybe it was the teachers. But, hey, I'll never forget trying out. I'll never regret it. I only wish I would've done better. Spent a little more time. Oh, well. Life is life. Sometimes you'll win, sometimes you won't. But the only thing is, it wasn't my loss. It was theirs. They'll never know how good I could've been."

I'll admit that sometimes I can go a little overboard with the drama, but it really meant the *world* to me to win this election. For some reason, my happiness depended on it. I wish I could go back to that day and relive it, knowing what I know now! I've since learned that things are usually never as big of a deal as they seem.

At least I was right about one thing: "Life is life. Sometimes you'll win, sometimes you won't." But I've learned that the key is to be content with whatever outcome and to be grateful for each day and each opportunity.

President Thomas S. Monson said, "We can lift ourselves, and others as well, when we refuse to remain in the realm of negative thought and cultivate within our hearts an attitude of gratitude." (Thomas S. Monson, "An Attitude of Gratitude," *Ensign*, May 1992, 54)

Eventually I got over the trauma of not making Student Body Office, and instead of wallowing in self-pity, I began to work really hard to develop my talents. I started taking singing lessons from Dean Kaelin, one of the best vocal coaches in Utah. I had learned to play the piano when I was six, and had always just read the music in front of me. But pretty soon I could hear a song on the radio, and then come home and pick it out by ear.

I also decided to start taking guitar lessons. The first song I learned was Faith Hill's "Breathe." I have to admit, that even to this day I *hate* practicing the guitar! Mainly just because the strings hurt my fingers. But my parents insisted that in order to be taken seriously as a country singer, I needed to learn how to play the guitar, so practice I did until my fingers blistered.

I competed in several talent shows and learned how to entertain an audience. I even won first place in a competition for adults at a multi-county fair called Westfest, yodeling LeAnn Rimes' "Cowboy's Sweetheart."

I even wrote my very first song entitled "All of Mine" which ended up being the song I auditioned with for the Salt Lake Idol competition several years later!

Before I knew it, I advanced to the Mia Maids in Young Women's, and my testimony grew even stronger. I was asked to be the President of my Mia Maid class after a few months, and loved serving the other girls.

Some of my very favorite memories are going to Girls Camp. During my first year at Stake Camp, we had a faith walk on the last night. At each station, we were told a pioneer story by leaders dressed all in white. They looked like angels in the moonlight. My mom was there, and told a story about one of my ancestors. The veil seemed so thin that night, and it strengthened my testimony permanently.

Ninth grade year was my most awkward year of Junior High. I had serious acne (in fact, a boy in my math class even called me "pimple cheeks!") my body was . . . let's just say *underdeveloped,* and I was extremely shy around boys. To make matters worse, all of a sudden my friends started leaving me out—again! I couldn't understand what it was about me that was so un-likeable. The more I tried to corner them and ask them what in the world I did wrong, the more they began to avoid me.

One night I overheard one of my friends talking to her mom, complaining about how much I was bugging her. I had planned on staying the night, but immediately called my mom to have her come get me after hearing that. I have no idea why my friends began acting like they were "too good" for me, but I also knew that as much as I tried, there was nothing I could do about it. My mom frequently told me to just make new friends, but it was hard when I had spent almost every waking moment for the past three years with those girls.

But being on the "outside" actually became beneficial to me. I began to get to know new people and realized that sometimes the "popular" kids weren't actually the nicest kids. In fact, one of my very best friends who I'm still close to was also one of the "un-popular" kids. She was always there for me and one day, as I was lamenting about how sad my life was, she said, "Carmen, I've learned to let things go and forgive people no matter how rude they've been to me. If you let things bother you, then you'll never have a fun year." Her advice hit home, and really helped me put things in perspective. I tried to take it to heart and even though my friends didn't really change, my attitude did.

While all of my old friends applied for Bountiful High School at the end of our ninth grade year, I made a prayerful decision to attend the rival school (which Camille also attended, and *promised* me I'd love) and get a fresh, new start at Woods Cross High.

At left, I am with my big sister Camille when I was just a few weeks old. Then at the right, I am a few months older and a lot happier!

Caught! My first attempt at applying lipstick didn't go very well.

'Sup, dude? Here I am looking stylish on a trip to the store.

Camille and I outside our condo in Irvine enjoying a sunny day sitting on the porch.

Playing the piano on Christmas Eve.

I've always been a country girl at heart!

My first appearance at the Stadium of Fire— as a dancer.

Some of my first performances— singing in the basement of the Bountiful Library.

My first "Glamour Shot" in the apricot orchards behind my dad's clinic. This was right around the time I was making the transition from Primary to the Young Women program, ready to become a busy (and beautiful) Beehive!

My first day of seventh grade—and the big step to junior high!

Showing off my new braces at cheer camp in 8th grade.

I had a great time as a member of the cast of Joseph and the Technicolor Dreamcoat. Donny Osmond treated us all so well, and I loved the excitement of being on stage. (I think my mom enjoyed taking this photo more than I enjoyed posing for it!)

Durng my 8th grade year, I was a cheerleader for Mueller Park Junior High This is the first—and only—time I did the splits for a photo.

This was one of those days as a teenager when you really wish that your family would just put the camera away.

CHAPTER FOUR

My "Wild" Years

"In the next [3] years you will make some of your sweetest memories and grow inside and out so much. The first thing to remember is that to be happy, you have to first know who you are and what you stand for. If you aren't happy deep inside, no outside factors will matter."

—A Sweet Sixteen letter from my sister, Camille, March 2001

I was really excited about being a WX Wildcat, and decided to try out for the cheerleading team again, mainly to make new friends. I ended up making it, and loved the girls on the squad. Most of them already knew each other from South Davis Junior High, but they included me, and pretty soon, it was like I'd known them all my life. Finally, I felt like I had a good group of friends again. I *knew* I made a good decision to go there!

At the Homecoming assembly, us cheerleaders were asked to perform a cheer and a dance. We did pretty well, but afterward as we were all rallying off stage, I got a little over-enthusiastic about showing my new school spirit, and kept kicking and cheering—BY MYSELF—oblivious to the fact that my fellow teammates were already hurrying off the stage.

When I finally turned around, I ran smack into a big blue thing: the curtain. I was so embarrassed! Everyone started laughing. Several people whistled at me, and someone yelled "Uh-oh!" as I frantically ran up and down the stage, smacking the curtain with both of my hands, trying to find the opening. Finally, I gave up on it and trying to make a joke, I put both hands over my mouth in an "Oh!" gesture, did one last little kick and bolted between the space where the wall and curtain met. I shoved my way past the band members who were waiting their turn backstage, pushing through the tubas and trumpets back to the dressing room, completely mortified.

An hour later, in one of the bathrooms, a girl looked over at me and said, "Aren't you the girl who got lost in the curtain?" And that was my lasting impression of being a Woods Cross cheerleader.

I also decided to try out for Madrigals (the honor choir) at the end of my sophomore year. I thought it would be so fun to sing in the choir that my older sister used to sing in. But I didn't end up making it. I was stunned. Singing was what I did best! I couldn't believe it. I wanted to be in choir so badly, but because I didn't make Mads, I didn't sign up for any other choir classes. It would be that or nothing, so I decided I just had to better prepare myself and try again the following year.

I also decided to try out for our school play. I didn't make the lead, but that was fine with me. I felt I was just paying my dues until senior year when I was promised by the drama coach herself that she'd cast me as the lead.

Sophomore year I was a Shark dancer in *West Side Story* and junior year I was a wife in *The King and I*. Even though I still didn't have any major parts, I loved getting up on stage, and despite my nerves, always looked forward to performing.

Some exciting events happened at the end of my sophomore year. For one thing, I got my driver's license—*barely*! I didn't have room in my schedule to take Driver's Ed, so I ended up talking private lessons. On the day of my test, I ran over the curb three times before finally making it out of the parking spot! I passed the test with one point to spare.

I also began dating. A boy named Adam asked me out for my first date as soon as I turned 16 to a concert (which was held in our high school auditorium), and then out for frozen custard. I had a lot of fun, especially because we went with two other couples we were friends with. It was snowing that day, and on the way home, Adam asked me if it was okay that he drop me off at the top of my street, because he didn't want to get stuck at the bottom. It *was* a steep road, but I didn't feel like walking down by myself in the dark! Luckily, he was gentleman enough walk me down the snowy sidewalk—in his sandals!

Finally I was old enough to advance to the Laurel class, and to my delight, my mom was called as the Young Women President. I loved having her in with me, and she was extremely supportive and encouraged me to get my Young Women Recognition award. I was so happy the day I finally received it!

It was a lot of hard work, and at times I wondered why I was doing it, but I will forever be grateful I did. It is a wonderful symbol to me of faith and hard work. It was a great way to set goals and it helped prepare me for my future as a wife, mother, and daughter of God. If you've ever wondered whether or not it's worth it to go ahead and try for it, let me tell you from experience—it *definitely* is!

We also began to talk more about responsibility, chastity, and morality in our Laurels class, and how important it was to stay clean and pure.

♪ ♪ ♪

Individual Worth

Let me tell you something I've learned specifically about kissing. Sure, it's great. I will even go as far as to say it's *awesome*! There's nothing wrong with just that—a kiss. But when you go from a sweet, goodnight kiss to passionate kissing, it's really easy to get into trouble.

My sister gave me some great advice about boys on my sixteenth birthday. She said, "[Boys] will respect you if you respect yourself." Girls, it's true. You are worth waiting for!

I always promised myself I'd stay clean and pure before marriage. At the end of my junior year, I was dating a boy named Jack. He was very good looking, funny, and had a bit of a wild streak to him. I used to love riding in his huge car and making all the other girls jealous of my smokin' hot boyfriend and his equally smokin' hot car. What made it even better, was that he was from a different school.

I don't know what it was about dating someone from a different school, but for some reason it felt like a very rebellious thing to do, which made it all the more exciting. One night, before Jack dropped me off, we went to the bottom of my street to "look at the view."

We had the radio on, and I knew what was coming—he was going to kiss me. In that moment, it was suddenly clear to me that what my parents and Young Women's leaders had always tried to warn me about was true—it's much easier to avoid a bad situation all together than to try to get out of it!

He leaned in, and as soon as the initial butterflies subsided, a queasiness seeped in. All of a sudden, I knew I needed to go home—NOW. I felt very uncomfortable, but I didn't know what to do, or how to tell him how I felt. Mid-kiss, I suddenly just said the first thing that came to my mind: "Goodnight!"

He stopped and just looked at me. Then he slowly started the car, drove up to my house, and dropped me off. I heaved a huge sigh of relief when I stepped into the house. Nothing happened. But because I put myself in a bad situation, something very well could have. I strongly disagree with even putting yourself in a situation that you know is questionable. The best thing to do is avoid it all together. But if you ever do find yourself in a bad situation, do the next best thing and GET OUT!

I'll always be grateful I listened to the quiet, urgent promptings of the spirit and got myself out. Years later, when I met my husband, he told me that one of the things that most attracted him to me was the fact that I had kept myself clean and pure. I saved the most sacred, beautiful part of myself for him—and only him.

Kisses are so special and intimate, and not until I was married did I fully realize how special and intimate they really are. You will never regret making a right choice. No matter how much you're made fun of, no matter if you get dumped, ridiculed, or laughed at, it will always be worth it.

The guy pressuring you into doing something you know is wrong IS NOT the guy you want standing beside you in the future! The man to marry is the man who respects you and who respects himself, because that is the man who will treat you like the daughter of God you are.

Stick to your guns, girls! And then, when you finally meet the man of your choice, he'll thank you for saving yourself for him. You are both worth it!

CHAPTER FIVE

Salt Lake Idol

"Carmen, what have you got to lose?"
                                —My dad's response after my initial
                                reluctance to send in an audition tape

Before I knew it I was a big bad senior. Here is my journal entry after my first day of school that year.

Aug. 26, 2002

Today was my last first day of school! It's so crazy being one of the old ones! I actually had to ask the administrator where my 1st period class was—how funny is that! I felt like a Sophie again. I wore a black V-neck 3-quarter length top and my new Dickies. I looked HOT! I loved my AP Art History class! I am so excited—I'm gonna have so much fun!!!

I saw Joe on my way to physics, and we both like, stuck our hands out at the last min. to say "hi" and I grabbed onto his finger, and we squeezed! It was so cute!!! I have a secret crush on him . . . So then physics was w/Ben and Brennen and I heart them! They truly act like my friends now. And Ben put his arm around me! Oh, I like him, too. Oh, and guess how cute this is. Derek carried my

AP Art History book for me since it weighed like 50 pounds! How cute is that!

I had to go to work from 3 pm to 6, and Mom forgot to put my stuff in the wash! So, I wore my little sis' shirt, and turned my dirty apron backwards. So then I cleaned my room and painted my nails in a french manicure. Well, I better go to sleep—I have school tomorrow! WEIRD! I still can't believe that I'm a senior. It hasn't hit me yet. Aaaah! I luv Matt! I luv Joe! I luv Ben! I luv Brennen!

Luv, Carmen

Those first few weeks of my senior year flew by without any major glitches. I was on the Dance Company, I finally made Madrigals at the end of my junior year, I was getting decent grades, and I had a really good group of friends who were trying to live the gospel standards as I was.

I also had a crush on every single boy who went to my school, and apparently, was no longer having confidence issues. Looking back, life seemed pretty easy at the time. I was getting ready to apply for college, and was hoping to possibly make the lead in the play that year. Then I heard the shocking news that the school wasn't going to be putting on a play.

I couldn't even wrap my mind around that. Woods Cross High was known for it's amazing college-level productions, and my sister was the lead her senior year, performing to sold-out crowds every night. It was what I always thought I'd be doing when I was her age. Everything I had done up to that point was to prepare myself for that major audition. But unfortunately, the drama department didn't make enough money the year before to have that privilege, so we wouldn't be able to put on a play.

Disappointed, I focused my time on choir and dance and soaking in every last minute of high school. I even got a job, and was known as what is affectionately called a "scoopie" at Nielsen's

Frozen Custard up in Bountiful. It's pretty self-explanatory. Basically, I scooped custard. Yup, life was pretty rough.

Then one fall day, my world was flipped upside down like a pancake and would never be the same again.

It all began with a piggy-back ride. The boy who was carrying me, Derek, was very tall and lanky. All of a sudden, one of our goofy friends thought it would be funny to see if he could get me to fall off, and began to hit Derek. He began to dart this way and that, oblivious to my screams as I flailed around on top.

Inevitably, he lost his balance and dropped me. Down I came, landing awkwardly on my right foot. (First mistake: Riding piggy-back atop a 6'3" person. Second mistake: Trusting my safety to a high school boy.)

"Oh my heck, are you okay?" Derek asked, helping me up.

"Uh, I think so," I stammered, trying to keep my voice steady. In all honesty, I'd never felt such pain in my life. It felt like my foot was on fire. It even had it's own heartbeat.

"It's okay, Der," I finally said. "I just need to get home."

I hobbled over to the car and started it up. As soon as I shut the car door, I began to bawl my eyes out. Driving home was a challenge. It was hard to see the road through my tears. Halfway to my house, I reached down to feel my throbbing foot at a stoplight. My eyes almost popped out my head when I thought I felt a bone sticking straight out of the side of my foot.

I was shaking so badly by the time I got home that I thought I'd pass out. I pushed through the back door and hopped to the couch, wailing.

"Carmen! What's wrong?" My mom quickly hung up the phone with my grandma, and hurried to kneel beside me.

"I'm dying!" I screamed. Well, not really, but that's what it felt like. Turns out, I had a badly sprained foot, and what I thought was bone sticking out were merely muscles that had spazzed out (like me) and formed a rock-solid ball because of the impact. But besides being grossly huge and all sorts of black and blue, my foot was going to be okay. I was going to live.

The next day, I stayed home from school. I felt miserable. I couldn't even walk on my foot, and I spent the morning on the couch watching TV and feeling sorry for myself.

Around 3 p.m. the phone rang. I was not going to haul myself up to get it, but for some reason I couldn't just sit there, so I needlessly yelled, "I'm coming!" as I awkwardly hobbled over to the phone.

"Hello?" I answered. Except it sounded more like, "HELLO!"

"Hey, Carmie!" my dad said. "Whatcha doin?"

"Being miserable."

"Oh. Well, guess what? A nurse here at the hospital just told me that *American Idol* auditions are today! You remember that show? All you have to do is videotape yourself singing a song a cappella and send it in to FOX 13 by 5:00 tonight! I think you should do it! What do you think?"

Whoa. Hold on. *What?*

"Dad, of course I would like to try out, but I'm in my pajamas with a huge boot on my foot. We don't even own a video camera, and the tape is due in two hours. How am I supposed to do that?"

Then my dad said something that I'll never forget: "Carmen, what have you got to lose?"

He was right. I felt a surge of excitement as I glanced once more at the clock. I wanted to do this. I immediately hung up and got to work. First came Plan A: I called my Grandpa. But for some odd reason, his video camera wasn't working.

Then came Plan B: I called my friend Katie. She told me to come on over. "Yeah right," I said, looking down at my foot. But this was *American Idol* we were talking about, so I stuffed myself in the car, said a prayer, and somehow made it up to her house. As I was coming up the driveway, she opened the front door and said, "Carmen, I'm so sorry, but I just realized, we don't have any tapes left!"

Okay. Don't panic. Time for Plan C! I called another friend, and she told me that she did have tapes, a camera, and to come on over. Once again, I got back in the car, said another prayer, and drove (miraculously) to my friend Becca's house. It was now 3:45 p.m., and I was losing precious time.

"Okay," I said, trying desperately to make myself look presentable in blue PJs with a Pebbles ponytail on top of my head. Not to mention, of course, the big, black boot on my right foot—and hardly any make-up.

"What song should I sing?" I asked Becca. "Where should we film it?"

"Hmmm." Becca thought for a minute. "Oh, I know! You can sit on my parents' bed. The sun is shining in there. And then we'll do another take against the wall in the family room."

Right. Bed, wall, family room. Very glamorous. Becca quickly filmed me singing the first verse and chorus of "All of Mine" (the song I wrote when I was 14) and then we went into the living room to transfer it to a tape. Besides an awkward close-up of just my nose, Becca actually didn't do too bad as a camerawoman.

"Uh, oh . . . " Becca said slowly after the tape finished.

"What?" I asked. "What's 'uh, oh'? We don't have time for 'uh, oh!'"

"Um . . . well . . . the cord that connects the camera to the VCR is up at Brennen's house. I forgot I let him borrow it."

Once again! In the car! Up to Brennen's! By now, I was a pro at driving with a boot on (although I wouldn't recommend it). It was 4:15 when we arrived, and just to add to my stress, we rang the bell and no one was home. "Hey!" Becca called to me from around the side of house. "The back door's open! Let's go!"

Now she was really getting into the spirit of things, and ever the enthusiast, I followed her around the house and into the basement. Telling myself that it was for *American Idol* and that Brennen would surely understand if we were discovered in his home, I rummaged around until I found the cord. We plugged everything in and began recording on his TV downstairs.

I checked the clock again. 4:30 p.m. I had exactly thirty minutes to finish the tape and drive down to the hospital where my dad was meeting me to run it out to the local FOX studios. I was now officially freaking out.

Meanwhile, Brennen and some of our guy friends showed up. "Hey . . . Carmen? Becca? How did you guys get in—"

"It's for *American Idol.*" I interrupted. As I was watching the tape back, I was suddenly self-conscious about everyone watching my silly performance—including my up-close-and-personal nose shot. Finally, the tape was ready.

I yelled goodbye, walked as fast as my gimpy legs would carry me to my car, drove down to the hospital, and handed the tape out the window to my dad who was waiting for me in the hospital's parking lot on his motorcycle. He sped off, I drove home. Later that night, he told me he drove 90 miles per hour on the freeway to get it out to FOX in time. As soon as he handed the tape to the man waiting outside the studio, the man held it up and said, "This will be the last tape we're accepting today!" Talk about just in the nick of time.

I talked on the phone to one of my friends that night, explaining in detail how I probably looked and sounded on camera. Pretty soon, doubts started to creep into my mind. Thoughts like, "They're not going to pick me—I'm not good enough." By the end of the night, I had convinced myself that I wasn't going to make it. I cried to my mom about how horrible I must have looked and sounded. I must've been pretty convincing to her, because instead of staying home on Friday to wait for a call-back, she went to Ogden with my grandma to go shopping. Luckily, I had given FOX my cell phone number, just in case.

That day I was sitting in the school theater watching my teammates dance onstage when my phone rang. My heart froze. I didn't recognize the number. Could it be . . . ?

"Hello?"

"Hi, is this Carmen Rasmusen?"

I almost screamed with joy. "Yes, it is."

"Hi, Carmen, I'm calling to let you know that you've made call-backs for the Salt Lake Idol auditions. Can you come to Salt Lake tomorrow to audition for the second round?"

I couldn't contain myself anymore, and as soon I told him yes and hung up, I let out a loud "Whoo-hoo!" I had made it! Pajamas, boot, weird song, granola face and all. I was totally ecstatic.

Saturday came way too soon, and before I knew it, I was in Salt Lake, waiting for my name to be called to audition. My dad had panicked the night before about my "image" and insisted that I duct-tape my foot instead of wear my boot. So, trying to act as normal as possible, I walked very carefully into the audition room as soon as my name was called.

I sang "Blue" by LeAnn Rimes—my signature song. The audition went really well, and I ended up making it to the final round. There were five of us remaining. After we had each auditioned for the judges a second time, they gathered us together, and threw us all for a loop. Instead of announcing the winner that day, they were going to highlight one of our auditions each day throughout the following week. Then on Friday, we would all go on the FOX morning show together and they would announce the winner live.

They also told us all to pack our bags, because the winner would have to leave for Los Angeles early Saturday morning. I couldn't believe they were going to drag out the decision. I guess they didn't mind if we all went crazy with anticipation!

Monday, Tuesday, Wednesday, and Thursday all seemed to drag by. Each day I'd turn on the TV, hoping it would be the day that they aired my audition, and each day I'd end up disappointed. Finally, Friday rolled around.

Surprisingly, I felt really peaceful as we drove down to the FOX studios that morning. I joined the other waiting contestants at the table in the back room, and I finally saw my audition on TV. It was weird to see myself performing, and I thought I sounded different. But I still felt good about it, and was really hoping that there was a reason they saved me for last.

My mom just kept smiling as she helped me get ready in the studio restroom before we went on camera. She said, "I know you're meant to do this. I just feel like you're supposed to."

Finally, we were all called into the newsroom. They lined us up in a row in front of the camera, asked each of us a few questions, and then finally the announcer said, "The person we've chosen to be the Salt Lake Idol is . . . "—and I saw the camera fall on me—"Carmen Rasmusen!"

I had a beauty queen moment and screamed. I was so unbelievably excited! All that work (and all that pain) had been worth it. My friends had all been watching, and they started calling me one after the other, screaming and telling me that they wanted to take me out for dinner that night to celebrate. I couldn't keep the smile off my face.

That afternoon as I we pulled up to the school to pick up my homework and tell my teachers I might be gone for awhile, I was suddenly bombarded with students running up to me, telling me how "cool" it was that I had made it. I guess the news had spread like wildfire, and pretty soon the whole school knew about it. I remember walking down the halls with people shouting out "Congratulations!" as I walked by. For the first time, I felt like I was on my way.

That night, my friends and I went out to eat at the Hard Rock Cafe in downtown Salt Lake. They told our waitress that I had just been chosen as the Salt Lake Idol, and she invited me to sing my audition song for the entire restaurant. So I climbed atop a glass case displaying one of Elvis' performing outfits and belted out "Blue."

It was so cool! My friends all made me a huge card, and threw a party for me afterward. It all felt so surreal. The feelings of anticipation, excitement, and pure joy stayed with me throughout that night. I remember looking up at the stars, wishing that feeling would never end. My dream was finally coming true.

CHAPTER SIX

Hollywood!

"That was ghastly."
—Simon Cowell's first impression of me

The morning after I was named the Salt Lake Idol, I flew out to Los Angeles with Lane Lyon (a news reporter from FOX), a cameraman, and my mom. I was now their new "story." I was a story! I walked through the airport with the camera in my face and felt everyone's eyes on me. It was weird and awesome at same the time. I felt like a star!

Everything about the first trip out to California was magical. As soon as we landed, we drove to the hotel to check in and relax for awhile before going off to film a news segment for the night. I admit I was a little surprised to pull up to a Best Western in Hollywood, but it turned out that a lot of legendary movie stars had once stayed there. It was actually very cool.

Each room number had a star around it, and it felt so neat to be staying in a place that actresses such as Lucille Ball had stayed. To make it all the more perfect, as we pulled out to go eat, we noticed the sign on the corner said "Carmen Avenue." We were staying on the corner of Carmen Avenue! I couldn't believe it. "It's a sign!" I said.

That night at dinner, something unusual happened. I got up to go to the bathroom, and as I was waiting in line, I absentmindedly began to hum a tune. One of the waiters passed me, and asked, "Are you a singer?"

"I hope I will be, someday," I replied.

Later, as the same waiter was pouring our water at our table, he said, "I have a feeling about you. What are you here for?"

"The *American Idol* auditions."

"You're going to make it," he said. That threw me off guard, but I was very pleasantly surprised. Wow. Another sign!

That night, Lane Lyon took us to the corner of Hollywood and Highland to film another news segment. I walked down the Hollywood Walk of Fame and stopped at the entrance to the Kodak Theatre—the place where the *American Idol* finale was held. I closed my eyes and imagined myself singing on stage there, with hundreds of fans screaming my name. I could almost believe it.

Afterward, we drove to the Rose Bowl in Pasadena to see where I would be auditioning. I was stunned. There were 5,000 people camped out and waiting in line to audition. I couldn't believe how many people were there! Sleeping bags, blankets, and make-shift tents were everywhere, and the sound was incredible! EVERYONE was singing! They were all hoping that maybe this time, their dreams would come true.

We found out that some people had been camping out for several days, and they were going to have to get ready in the parking lot the morning of the audition. I was suddenly very grateful for my room in the Best Western.

The day before the audition, something very traumatic happened. I broke a nail. I was so upset! I had just received a manicure, and I simply couldn't imagine auditioning unless I got the nail fixed. Luckily, we found a little beauty salon several blocks from our hotel. I sat down and began to make small talk with the manicurist.

"So, have you ever done a famous person's nails?" I asked.

"Oh, yes," she mentioned casually. "I do a lot of famous people's nails. In fact, Paula Abdul comes in here frequently to get hers done."

My mom and I slowly looked at one another with the same thought: *Paula Abdul gets her nails done from the same lady that was now doing mine?* How many more signs did we need?! I now felt for sure that this was meant to be.

Before I knew it, the morning of the auditions had arrived. I had to get up really early to do my hair and make-up, and I had to do several live shots with FOX. To say I was nervous is a serious understatement. I was terrified. *How in the world is anyone going to get through?* I wondered. *And how are they going to remember us all?* I got my answer soon enough.

After about four hours of waiting and being herded from one room to the next, I was finally waiting outside the first audition door. My number was 13171. (This was also a good sign—7 was my lucky number!) I walked in with the rest of my group and saw a producer and a cameraman sitting at a table across from us, waiting to send us through or send us packing.

When our number was read, we were to step forward and begin singing. Some people sang a line, some sang about three notes. Luckily, I was one of the line singers. I was still nervous, but also confident. I stuck with my tried-and-true "Blue." My whole group was asked to leave except me.

Yes! I made it! I thought. But it wasn't over yet.

"All, right. Carmen?" The producer looked at the sheet of paper in front of him with my information on it. "Tell me something unique about yourself."

What? I wasn't supposed to be talking. Ask me to sing more! "Um . . . I play the guitar!" I announced proudly.

"Nope, that's not unique enough," he said. "Tell me something more unique about yourself."

Now feeling suddenly nervous and unsure of myself, I said, "I . . . uh . . . I . . . like to write songs!" Please let that be unique enough!

"Still not unique enough," the producer said. "C'mon, Carmen. I want to know something that makes you unique."

By this time, my hands were sweating and I could feel tears forming behind my eyes. I desperately racked my brains for anything unique, but at the moment I felt like I was the most boring person in the world. I had to get control of myself, or I was going to lose it.

Suddenly, an idea popped into my mind that was very weird and bizarre, but before I could really think about what I was saying, I blurted, "Um, I can talk with my mouth closed!"

The producer looked up and smiled. "Show me."

So, I closed my mouth, puffed out my cheeks and said, "Um, I can talk like this!"

Still smiling, he handed me a blue piece of paper. "Okay. You're through. Go on upstairs for the next audition." I was shocked. Why in the world did that weird talent put me through? But obviously not wanting to argue about his decision, I took the paper, thanked him and headed upstairs to where there were not as many people waiting for my next audition. After about five minutes, someone asked me what room I was assigned.

"Number 1," I said, looking at my paper.

"Oh, no," they replied. "They're really tough in there. *No one* has been getting through from room Number 1." At that moment, the door opened and a boy walked out, shaking his head. I was horrified.

"Next!" Someone shouted from inside. I couldn't move. I was now terrified of room Number 1. Forcing my legs forward, I threw back my shoulders and faked complete confidence as I entered the room. I took a quick look around, and to my surprise, everyone was smiling at me. I took a shaky breath and began to sing my song. They kept smiling, and I began to think that maybe they weren't so bad after all. Then, the one with the British accent (who happened to be Ken Warwick, producer of *American Idol*) said, "Yes, darling. You're through!"

Absolutely elated, out I came, now with another paper in hand. My mom was right there waiting for me, and she wrapped me in a huge hug. We walked downstairs to a little desk and I turned in my paper for another one—one that said I was to come back on Thursday. That was when the real auditions began—in front of judges Paula Abdul, Randy Jackson, and of course, the dreaded Simon Cowell.

I had never watched Simon give his famous criticism. In fact, the first episode of *American Idol* I ever saw was the Season 1 finale when Kelly Clarkson won. I must admit the only reason I watched it was because my friend Corrine called and said, "Turn on your TV to FOX and look at this girl's hair. Do you think I could do mine like that?"

So really, I had no idea what the show was about or what it would be like to actually perform in front of the judges.

Before I flew out to Los Angeles, my aunt printed me off a sheet from the Internet with all the contestants' names and what songs they sang from the first season, so that I would have an idea of what I was getting myself into, and also so I could answer any questions I was asked about the first season.

Thursday came much too soon. Again, I woke up early and did my hair and make-up the exact same way I had on Monday. We were also told to wear the same outfit we wore on the day of our first auditions to help them remember who we were. It turns out that was also what our "weird" talents were for, so they could look at us and say, "Carmen . . . Carmen . . . oh yeah, you're the one who can talk with her mouth closed!"

There were now about 250 people left—talented and otherwise. I sat next to an interesting person named Roxy who had on a mini-skirt, lots of sparkly make-up and a beautiful wig. Clearly, he was confused about his gender. There was also a cute blonde girl who called herself a witch.

I felt like I was suddenly auditioning for the circus. That suspicion was confirmed when I opened the door to the bathroom and out walked Dorothy from *The Wizard of Oz*. *Wow. I'm* definitely *not in Utah anymore*, I thought.

Finally, it was my turn to go audition. I was very shaky as I walked into the room. I couldn't believe I was about to meet the famous Simon, Paula and Randy! My stomach was doing flip-flops. But as it turned out, only Paula and Simon were there waiting for me. (Apparently, Randy was off shooting a Krispy Kreme commercial.) We said hello, and they asked me what song I was going to sing.

"I am going to sing 'Cowboy's Sweetheart,'" I announced proudly, thinking that it was a good choice of song since it showed off my yodeling skills.

"All right," Simon replied. "Whenever you're ready."

I sang through the entire first verse and chorus before stopping. Simon didn't even look up at me. The first words out of his mouth were, "Well, that was ghastly."

I suddenly wanted to laugh. In fact, I think I did.

"So, you're country, then?" he asked.

"Yes, I like country, but I like pop, too," I replied, hoping to sound versatile.

"Sing a pop song," Simon said. So, I sang "Supergirl" off of the *Princess Diaries* soundtrack. It was not very good.

Then Simon said, "Sing 'Blue.'" Ah, finally something I was comfortable with! I should've sang that all along. After I finished, he started talking about how he liked me, how I was unique and different, how he liked the fact that I was country. Honestly, I don't remember hardly anything else he said. I was too busy praying that I'd get through. Paula looked at Simon, then at me and said, "I'm on the fence."

"Oh, please. Please put me through!" I begged. They looked at each other one more time.

"It's a yes for me," Simon said, looking at Paula. She finally nodded and said "Yes" too. Then I heard the famous words: "It's a yes. Welcome to Hollywood."

"Thank you so much!" I gushed as I headed out the door. I was handed a gold piece of paper on my way out, and again, my mom was waiting for me. As soon as she saw the paper, she cheered. The camera was right there, filming it all, and after hugging my mom, I did a quick interview.

I was then led into another private room where I did another interview for *American Idol*. At the end, the lady conducting it said, "Okay. Could you now sing us a few lines from the theme song?" I froze. I didn't know the theme song! I had never even really watched the show!

"Um, no, that's okay. I don't really feel comfortable doing it," I said nervously, trying to escape from the chair.

She smiled and said, "No, really! Just sing a few lines like this, 'Ooo-whoa, ooo-whoa-ooo!'"

Mimicking her exactly, I quickly sang the lines back the way I heard them, and then bolted from the room. Later, as we were waiting to leave, producer Ken Warrick came up to me again. He congratulated me, and told me how much he liked me and my curly hair. He was so positive and encouraging.

We also saw Paula walking down the hall, I thanked her again, and she also said "Congratulations!" I was so happy. I couldn't believe that I was going back to Hollywood. Only a few more auditions, and I would be on the highest-rated TV show in the country, doing what I loved best. I was so close.

Posing among the autumn leaves with my family. From the left, Camille, me, Dad, Mom, Raquel and Robby.

I was feeling quite festive—and sparkly—during this performance around Christmas.

Christmas Eve with Camille, Robby, and Raquel.

As a sophomore at Woods Cross High School, I made the cheerleading squad. One of my favorite memories was getting all dolled up for glamour pictures by Hazen Photography.

As a junior, I had a blast as a member of The Dance Company.

By the time I was in high school, I was singing fairly often at local events and competitions. In this photo I am singing the National Anthem at an assembly for our school.

I loved getting into character in the play The King and I as a junior.

I was blessed to be a part of a great group of Young Women, and I was fortuante that Mom was one of our leaders. From clockwise left, Ashley, Erin, Melanie, Carly, my mom, me, and Amberley.

After being named the Salt Lake Idol, I crashed on the couch, and my family thought they would join me.

This is the day my life changed. I was heading to Hollywood!

CHAPTER SEVEN

On Second Thought...

*"It was a great experience, but I wouldn't try out
again."*
　　　　—My famous last words to FOX 13 right before I
　　　　was called back to try out for the "Wildcard" show

My experience during *American Idol's* Hollywood Week was
nothing like my first trip to Los Angeles. It was much, much
worse.

As the auditions progressed, the 256 contestants trying out
were cut in half each day until the top 32 were chosen. It was
now crunch time. Everyone was in it to win it.

We first had to audition in groups of five, and I was placed
in a group with a huge man with an equally huge voice named
Ruben Studdard. He was very friendly and super talented. Little
did we know that a few weeks later we'd be in the Top 12 together,
and then he'd eventually go on to win the competition.

During this audition, we were to pick any song of our choice.
I chose to sing a Carol King song, "I Feel the Earth Move." After
our performances, we all stood in a line, and one by one they
called on our numbers to either step forward or stay where we

were. I knew that I had a strong chance to make it through the first round, because Ruben was standing in the same line I was. Sure enough, we heard, "Front line, congratulations. You've made it through another round of auditions."

The next day, the judges decided to give us a challenge: we were to write music to lyrics they gave us and then perform our arrangement for our audition. That day was horrible! We waited hours to audition, and when we were finally called in, they announced they were going to break for lunch. While we were waiting, we made up a silly dance. When the judges finally came back from lunch, we performed our little routine onstage to help ease our nerves. Ruben and I ended up making it through that round as well.

The third day of Hollywood Week we were split into two groups—girls and boys. We were then asked to pick from among three songs, and then form groups of three with people who had chosen the same song. I chose "Don't Cry Out Loud," which has since become my least favorite song of all time and to this day makes me nauseated whenever I hear it playing.

The girls in my group were pretty good vocalists, but they weren't really into practicing. I remember trying to come up with simple moves with them behind the theater, right before our audition. Finally, we were called in. I hadn't been getting much advice from the judges up until this point, and I really wanted to impress them. When it was our group's turn, I sang my heart out and received enthusiastic applause from the audience when I finished. But the judges weren't quite as friendly. Randy commented that I was the only one he really felt something from, but Simon didn't say a word, and Paula simply asked me if I had a cold.

I was shocked. "Um, I have a little bit of a stuffy nose," I answered, thinking of my allergies, but I didn't think it was that obvious. I actually thought I did pretty well, and didn't understand why none of them were complimenting me. I was very confused.

That night as we were waiting outside the theatre for the results, I began to seriously doubt my performance. I was feeling unusually nervous about what the judges had said, but as usual, my mom kept telling me over and over that I was meant to do this. She was always so good at boosting my confidence, and had been very helpful the last couple of weeks in so many ways, such as ironing my clothes so I could practice, making me hot lemon-honey water to loosen up my vocal chords, and massaging my shoulders before I went on stage.

Several people had actually commented on how nice she was, and how they wished their moms could be there, too. I felt so lucky to have her with me. My mom has always sacrificed so much for us, and that night as I listened to her talk about how much faith she had in me, I actually believed that I would make it through.

As we walked back into the theatre, they had us all sit down in rows. We were then asked to come up onstage when our name was read, and stand in the row we were assigned. I ended up being in the last row, and I knew right then and there that I wasn't going to make it. The girls standing next to me hadn't performed very well, or received positive comments from the judges. I felt my heart literally skip a beat as I heard, "Congratulations"—and then some girl beside me screamed, thinking that she had made it—"for making it this far . . . but your journey ends tonight. I'm sorry, but you're not going on."

I was going home. I glanced at my mom in the audience, and she looked like she was going to faint. It was wrong, all wrong. This couldn't be happening. I was supposed to make it. She said so! I had performed my best! What was going on? It felt like a dream, a horrible dream as I stood in line to receive my ticket home. I felt totally defeated, and I was mad. Nasty little thoughts started going through my mind about those contestants who had made it through. I was suddenly angry at each and every one of them, and especially everyone at *American Idol* who had led me on, letting me think I actually had a chance. I felt like someone had hit me in the stomach with a ton of bricks, and I couldn't shake the feeling. How was I going to return home and tell everyone I didn't make it? What was I going to say? That I wasn't good enough? *Was* I good enough? I sure didn't feel good at all.

The next few weeks were a blur to me. Luckily, it was so close to Christmas vacation that I had several days to unwind at home and pull myself together before going back to school. The holidays took my mind off of what had happened in Hollywood, but it also put a damper on my mood. I kept thinking how much better it would be if I had just made it to the next round.

Life was tough once school started again. Everyone asked me how my auditions went, but I was legally under contract and couldn't say anything until the show aired in January. So I'd just smile and say, "You'll have to see."

"Yeah, right!" they'd say. "We know you made it!" Those comments made things even worse.

There wasn't much to do but get on with my life. Every day, I had to convince myself it was for the best. And every day, my mom would look out the window for the FedEx truck, hoping they'd stop by our house with a package from FOX that said, "We're so sorry, but we made a mistake. Carmen really made it, and we want her back!" We were both stuck in a dream.

On the day the second season of *American Idol* premiered, Lane Lyon came back to my house to interview me and film me watching the first episode. By now, it was pretty clear to everyone that I hadn't made it. In the interview I said, "Oh, it was a great experience, but I wouldn't try out again."

It was really hard for me to talk about *American Idol* without angry feelings bubbling up inside. I couldn't watch it. I forbade my family from supporting it. But despite my protests, my little sister Raquel would not only watch the show every Tuesday and Wednesday night, she'd actually call in while the top 32 contestants were being chosen and *vote* for her favorites! I was furious! These were the same people that I had competed against—the ones that had beat me.

I remember watching the contestants' faces one night as Simon, Paula, and Randy announced that they were among the final 32 contestants. They were all so happy—like I should have been. All of a sudden, I just couldn't stand it anymore. Enough was enough. I was sick of these ugly, jealous feelings inside of me. I had always been taught to be happy for the success of others, but I was envious beyond anything I'd ever felt before, and it was eating me alive.

I marched into my parents' bathroom. I looked at myself in the mirror and really tried to imagine what it would have felt like had I made it. I closed my eyes and let myself *feel* it. Pretty soon, a huge smile spread across my face, and complete and utter elation poured from my head down to my toes. I started jumping up and down, screaming and clapping, turning around in circles, and shouting things like, "No way! I can't believe it! Oh my gosh!"

After about ten minutes of doing this (and receiving some very worried looks from family members who happened to walk by) something strange happened—I actually felt better! For whatever reason, me pretending to make it turned out to be very therapeutic, and for the first time in three months, I felt hopeful again.

Then a few days later, we received a phone call. A very interesting phone call. I had just gotten home from school when I heard the phone ring. My mom was in her bathroom getting ready when she answered it. She was on for quite awhile and was talking very animatedly. Pretty soon, I wandered in to see what all the fuss was about.

"Who are you talking to?" I mouthed silently. But she just grinned and shook her head. Finally, she hung up.

"So, who was it?"

"Guess . . . what," she said.

"What?"

"Guess what!"

"What?!"

"GUESS WHAT, GUESS WHAT, GUESS WHAT!" She exclaimed, grabbing my hands and jumping up and down.

"MOM! TELL ME! *WHAT?!*"

"That was Ken Warwick, the producer from *American Idol*. He wants you to come back and try out for the Wildcard show."

It was like deja vu. I turned around and just stared at myself in the mirror. All of a sudden, a huge smile spread across my face, and complete and utter elation poured from my head down to my toes. I started jumping up and down, screaming and clapping, turning around in circles, this time with my mom, both of us shouting things like "No way! I can't believe it! Oh my gosh!" This went on for several minutes as we soaked in this impossibly great news. Finally, we calmed down a bit and reality stepped in.

"So, when do we leave?" I asked.

"Tomorrow morning." She picked up the phone again. "I think you should get your hair done, we need to get you a new outfit, how are your nails . . . ?"

All of a sudden, I was completely overwhelmed. Was I really going to go back to California to try out for *that* show again? The same one I had banned from our house? It was all too weird. And what were the chances that Ken Warwick actually *remembered* me and wanted me to come back and just so·happened to reach us at home, the day before we had to leave?

The timing was all too perfect, too ironic, especially because it happened not two weeks after I had acted out this exact scenario in this exact same bathroom. It was almost as if . . . I willed it to happen.

After my mom hung up the phone and left the room, I walked over to her bed and knelt down beside it. I had so much to be thankful for, and wanted my Heavenly Father to know that I knew His hand was in this. My prayers were answered—not in the way I originally thought they would be, but now I had suddenly been given another chance at my dreams. For that, I knew I what I had to do. I began to pray in earnest, with all the sincerity of my heart. I poured out my gratitude for this second opportunity. I thanked Him for this chance. And I made a promise.

"Please, Heavenly Father. If Thou wilt please just, let me make it this time, I promise Thee that I will make Thee proud. I will stick to my standards. I will stay true to the values I have been taught. I will wear modest clothing, and I'll try my hardest not to fall into temptation. I will do my best to be an example to those around me, and to those who may see me on TV. Please, Father in Heaven. I want this more than anything. I promise, I won't let Thee down."

I stayed on my knees for several minutes, savoring the peaceful feeling that had come over me. I knew that if I made a commitment beforehand, then when the temptations came it would be much easier for me to resist them.

I love this quote from Elder Dallin H. Oaks:

"Commit yourself to put the Lord first in your life, keep His commandments, and do what the Lord's servants ask you to do. Then your feet are on the pathway to eternal life. You do not know what will happen. Do your best on what is fundamental and personal and then trust in the Lord and His timing." ("The Right Thing at the Right Time," *New Era*, July 2005, 4)

I had faith that no matter what, if I tried my best to stay true to the gospel, then my Heavenly Father would guide and bless me. I truly felt His love for me. I was excited to go back to L.A. and try once more for a spot on *American Idol*. I felt I had been given this second chance for a reason. But had I known what kind of world I was about to be thrown into, I probably would've stayed on my knees for much, much longer . . .

CHAPTER EIGHT

The Wacky Wildcard Week

"I'm going to take a bit of a risk here, because the person that I've chosen I don't think sang to the best of their ability last night . . . But I heard something which I thought was unique."
—Simon Cowell, the night of the Wildcard results show

When I first returned to Los Angeles, everything seemed magical again. A big black limo picked my mom and I up and drove us to the Avalon hotel where we would be staying. This hotel was gorgeous! And very "Hollywood." Apparently, Lucille Ball had filmed a famous "pool shot" at the Avalon's pool. It was very old-fashioned and charming. It just *felt* right!

The next day we practiced with a vocal coach named Byrd. We were to pick a song that day to try out with, and I was having a hard time. Suddenly, Nigel Lythgoe, another producer of *American Idol*, came walking over and said, "Have you ever heard 'Think Twice' by Celine Dion?"

58

I hadn't, so Byrd found the music and I began to hum along while Michael O., the piano player, picked out the melody. I immediately fell in love with it, and everyone agreed that should be the song I sing.

Later that night back in my hotel room, I sat on the bed with a mini tape recorder in hand, going over and over and over the song until I had it memorized. I have never before, nor since, practiced a song with such intensity and dedication. I sat on that bed for hours perfecting every line.

The next day, all of the contestants sat in the dreaded "red room" backstage to await our turn to perform. We were already so nervous, and I for one couldn't wait to just get it over with. Pretty soon, we saw Nigel enter the room and start toward us. He was walking with someone else, and not until he got close did we realize who it was . . . Simon Cowell. Everyone gasped.

"Now, kids, don't be nervous," Nigel started, not knowing that his words were now falling on deaf ears. Don't be nervous? Had he *met* Simon Cowell? "He is not going to be judging you, he is just going to sit in and watch."

Everyone was now totally panic-stricken, and I had to try very hard to keep from hyperventilating. As if we weren't already worried about impressing the producers, now we had to worry about the most critical person in the world staring at us with that bored look he always has on his face as we poured our hearts out. I suddenly wanted to melt into the carpet and disappear.

Luckily *and* unfortunately, I didn't have to go first. It was a double-edged sword, because the first person was the guinea pig, but he or she also had the chance to set the bar really high and then relax while all the rest of us had to sweat it out until it was our turn. (And I'm a nervous-sweater; I'm usually soaked before I even step onstage!)

Finally, it was my turn. I walked on stage and waited for

my cue. As soon as I heard the music, I got into character. I sang from the bottom of heart, belted from my toes, and looked Simon straight in the eye. I even surprised myself at how well I did. I walked back into the red room, smiling, because I felt that all the hard work I put in had paid off.

We all filed upstairs to hear the results of who was going through to compete live on the actual show, and who was going to pack up their belongings and head home—again.

Nigel held up a piece of paper and gave a little speech about how well we all did. Then he began to read the names of those who made it. My name was the first one.

"Carmen Rasmusen . . . " *YES!* I was overjoyed. This time was different. I would now be performing on national television! In front of millions of people! I had made it!

Even if I got cut after the first round, I had made the show. I was about to make my singing debut on national television for all to see and hear . . . and criticize.

I spent the next week rehearsing and doing photo shoots for the *American Idol* website. One day, I didn't feel like getting ready, so I didn't shower, I wore an outfit that wasn't really my favorite, and my hair was a piece of work. Just my luck, I found out soon after I arrived at the CBS studios that we would be doing a photo shoot for the website that day! That also became the picture that many newspapers used. It was *not* my most attractive shot!

A few weeks later, I found that same picture in a hair magazine. There was a caption that explained technically how to "do your hair like Carmen!"—doing things like spraying it with gel to prep the strands, twisting the individual pieces with your fingers to form loose curls, and then setting it with pomade. Little did they know how simple it really was—I just rolled out of bed!

By this time, I had gotten to know some of the other contestants who had also been called back. I became friends with a girl named Olivia, who was my age. Because we were both still in high school and under 18, we had to do three hours of school together, Monday through Friday with a tutor. We would sit downstairs at the CBS studios in a little dressing room and "do our homework." In reality, we would write in our journals, play Scrabble, and talk about how weird our tutor was.

Clay Aiken and Kimberly Caldwell were also two of my favorites. They were always laughing and joking together, and were very nice to me.

One day, as we were all waiting around in the red room, I decided to finish up the journal entry I had started in "class." Clay saw me writing something and said, "What's that?" Before I could say anything, he leaped over and snatched the paper away from me.

"No! Give it back!" I yelled.

"Oh, come on," he said. "Who cares? It's not like I'm going to show anyone. I just want to see what you're writing."

I was so embarrassed, but he was actually complimentary about how descriptive I was in my writing. I think that's when Clay and I first became friends.

Later that week, we all went shopping on the famous Melrose street for outfits to wear on the show. There were all sorts of funky shops with equally funky outfits displayed inside. And all *very* pricey.

In a few hours, everyone had picked out their outfit for the Wildcard show—except me. I hadn't really told the wardrobe people what my standards were, and was a little hesitant to say anything in front of all the other contestants. I didn't want to make them feel bad because of the outfits they had chosen, and yet I wanted them to know who I was, and why I didn't want to dress immodestly. Every time one of the stylists would come up to me, holding up a mini-skirt or tube top, I'd say, "Oh, that's not really my color," or "Um, no thanks. I don't really like it." I could tell they were getting frustrated when everyone else had decided on an outfit and was ready to go, and I was still looking around.

Finally, I spoke up. "You know, I'm not really comfortable wearing anything low cut."

"Oh. Okay," they said.

"Or too tight," I continued. "Or too short. Or that's sleeveless. Or backless . . ."

For awhile, they just sat there staring at me. I could tell they were confused. But then, one of them said, "No problem. We'll get you something that you feel comfortable in."

I was so relieved. In fact, they told me that they respected me for wanting to dress modestly. They sent everyone else home, and spent the next few hours looking around for something modest for me to wear. I finally settled on a cream V-neck wrap shirt with pink flowers and pink bunchy capri pants. *Now* I was ready!

We spent the next few days rehearsing our songs and working with Byrd. I chose to sing the song "Can't Fight the Moonlight" by LeAnn Rimes for the Wildcard show. I wanted to sing a country song, and I felt like this one was a good crossover for TV. My own vocal coach from Salt Lake City, Dean Kaelin, even flew out to help me work on it. Again, I practiced over and over and felt pretty comfortable with it, except for some really high notes that Dean wanted me to hit. He seemed to have more confidence in me than I did in myself, and even though I nailed the notes in practice, I was afraid I might chicken out onstage when the show was live and there was so much pressure. I wanted to just play it safe.

The night of the Wildcard show, we were able to get our hair and make-up done by the pros. As I was finishing up, in walked Simon Cowell! My mom got all excited and wanted me to get my picture with him. I was terrified, as usual, but asked if I could take a picture with him anyway. He agreed, and for the first time, I felt somewhat . . . familiar with him. I can't say comfortable, but familiar. He was much more friendly with the contestants backstage than he was on camera.

Earlier that day, Byrd had us all move around in a circle and clap our hands while singing, "Don't be nervous . . . be focused!" I tried to repeat that in my head several times as I walked downstairs to the stage, but it just made things worse.

Waiting backstage was torture. All of the cameras and loud music and flashing lights freaked me out. Of course, I was already sweating and shaking so badly out of nervous habit, that even my teeth began to chatter. I thought I'd die every time the show went to a commercial break. The interview Ryan Seacrest (the host) did with me before I went onstage drained every last ounce of courage I had. Finally, it was my turn.

I walked out onstage, knowing that the judges were scrutinizing my every move. There were cameras all around me, moving up and down. I was told to focus on and follow the little red light that meant that camera was recording, as well as look at the judges every now and then. So many things to remember, on top of remembering my lyrics. I didn't have time to gather myself together and try to calm my nerves before the music started.

I had rehearsed. I had done vocal warm-ups an hour before. I had prayed, and prayed, and prayed. But for some reason, the voice that came out as soon as I opened my mouth was not the voice I had been training. It was very, very shaky. I physically could not make my voice do what I wanted it to do. This was *not* how I normally sang. I knew right then and there that I wouldn't be able to hit the high notes I had worked so hard at hitting. So, I just sang the song straight. No embellishments, no impressive high notes, just . . . a mediocre performance. Not terrible. But not *American Idol*-worthy.

I felt ridiculous as I walked to that dreaded "X" on the stage, marking the spot where we stood to be judged. I wanted to just get away from that place. It had somehow sucked all the confidence and charisma right out of me. My energy and excitement had completely vanished. I slowly brought my hands behind my back, looked up at the Simon, Paula, and Randy, and awaited the verdict.

Simon looked at me and said, "Well, as you know, we brought several of you back so you could have a chance to shine, and you didn't. It wasn't good enough. Sorry."

My heart dropped onto the floor when Simon said that. I couldn't think of anything to say, so I simply nodded and walked offstage. Once again, Ryan was waiting to do an interview with me. He asked my little sister, Raquel, who had come out with Camille to come sit by me for moral support. It took every last bit of dignity I had to keep from sobbing. In fact, I think my voice cracked a time or two while I was talking. I hated that I had let everyone see how vulnerable I really was. This was nothing like I had expected. I wanted to go home.

That night, I ordered pizza up in the hotel room with my family. They were so sweet and sensitive, and we let all of our emotions out, laughing and crying. We talked about the great experiences I had had, how neat it was that I had performed on national television, and how mean Simon Cowell was.

It felt good to have my family around me, buoying me up. Then, Camille said, "I felt like it was me up there getting criticized," and that started us bawling all over again. I didn't think I could take much more of this crazy emotional roller coaster. I WANTED OFF!

Because I had received such negative comments from the judges, I assumed that I wasn't going to make it. I packed all my bags and didn't even practice my song. It was useless to get my hopes up again. The day of the results show I got dressed, went into the hair and make-up room, and walked backstage, completely calm. I had made peace with the fact that I was going home. I quickly pushed away any thoughts that crept into mind about maybe still having even just a sliver of a chance.

Right before the show began, we were all arranged on the blue benches onstage. Each of the judges were to reveal their *one* pick and then they would reveal the one who America had picked. There would be four of us from the nine Wildcard contestants that would be chosen to be in the Top 12.

The show started, and Randy revealed his Wildcard pick. He chose Kimberly Caldwell. After she performed her song again, it was Paula's turn. She decided to pick Trenyce. She also sang her song once more. Finally, it was Simon's turn. He was beating around the bush, talking a lot, trying to build the anticipation, while Ryan did his best to coax the result out of him. Finally Simon said something that caught my attention.

"Now, I'm going to take a bit of a risk here, because the person I've chosen I don't think sang to the best of their ability last night . . ." My head shot up. I definitely didn't sing to the best of my ability. Simon continued on.

". . . but I heard something which I thought was . . . *unique.*" Unique! There was that word again! I heard him say that once to me before, the day he told me I was going through to Hollywood. My heart was beating out of my chest now. All of a sudden, that tiny sliver of hope I had tried so hard to push away came back. It really sounded like . . . like Simon was talking about *me.* I was seriously going to need some counseling after this!

"The person I've chosen . . . " My stomach leapt into my throat. I held my breath thinking, *No way. No way, no way, no way. He's seriously going to choose me. "* . . . is Carmen."

I threw my hands over my mouth and stood up. Clay immediately grabbed me and wrapped me in a huge hug, laughing and whooping for joy right along with me. After we embraced, I ran up to the judges table to hug each of them, and tell them thank you. Paula looked at me and said, "I bet you're thinking, 'What? Okay, well, whatever!' So, yeah! Whatever!" Interesting. I *was* actually thinking just that!

The music started again, and I sang through my song once more, probably even worse than I had the night I auditioned. But I didn't care. I had made it.

After the show, Paula came up to me and said something that made a little more sense. "Okay, this is it now. You're going to have to work harder then ever before. You've got to step it up a notch."

I knew that she was right. I made a goal right then and there to work my guts out so I could blow everyone away the next week.

One of the most vivid memories I have of the entire *American Idol* experience was walking back into the red room, and meeting the other finalists who had made the Top 12. We were all told to stand in a line until we were called on stage again to be introduced for the first time together. I walked to the back of the line, taking my place behind Rickey Smith. I remember him and Ruben congratulating me as I looked down at the red carpet feeling happier than I'd ever felt.

But my favorite memory is standing against the wall in the dressing room on the set of our first photo shoot and calling my dad to tell him the news. I decided to be sneaky and trick him.

"Hi, Dad," I said in a sad voice as soon as he picked up.

"Hi, Carmie dear!" He sounded very apprehensive. "How did it go?"

I could tell he was expecting the worst, so I paused for awhile to add to the suspense before I exclaimed, "I . . . MADE IT!"

I remember exactly how my dad sounded. "No, way!" His voice went all scratchy, and I have never heard him sound so excited before. I was so happy that I had made him proud, and couldn't stop smiling all day. At that moment in time, everything in my life seemed absolutely perfect.

CHAPTER NINE

Pressure

"Oh my gosh, I'm so surprised. I'm so surprised!"
—My comments to the *Deseret Morning News*
about being chosen as Simon's pick for the Top 12

Making it as a finalist on *American Idol* made me, quite literally, an overnight success. One day I was a normal girl, and the next day I was "famous."

Radio stations, TV stations, and newspaper reporters were suddenly all calling, wanting to interview me. I was in magazines and newspapers and on TV and billboards across the country. Suddenly, I was "somebody."

It was fascinating to see how differently I was treated just because people knew my name. All of a sudden old flames started calling me again, and people that I was somewhat acquainted with in school were quoted in papers saying that I was their "life-long friend."

I guess some people would kill for all that recognition and worldly praise, and I can't say that it didn't have somewhat of an effect on me. I suddenly understood why people became obsessed with show biz: the spotlight was dangerously addicting.

The praise, the fan mail, the status, the free *stuff*—all of it was overwhelming.

People magazine did several photo shoots with the Top 12 contestants before we competed on Tuesday night for the first time. They wanted to capture us as a group before we began getting kicked off one by one.

For one of the photo shoots, they wanted us all dressed in the color blue. We all filed into the hair and make-up room, where we were told our outfits they had picked out for us were hanging on a rack. I walked to the back of the room and began shuffling through the hangers, looking for the one that had my name on it. Finally, I found it.

I pulled the outfit off the rack very slowly, squeezing my eyes shut and holding my breath, praying that it would be modest. It wasn't. I blew out my breath in frustration. What was I going to do now? I walked up to the person doing hair, and asked if they knew if there were any other outfits available to wear besides the one they picked out for me.

"Not that I know of—just the one hanging on the rack behind your name."

Desperate now, I did the only thing I could think to do in a crisis situation: I called my mom.

"Carmen, did you say a prayer?" she asked as soon as I told her what my dilemma was.

"Yes, Mom, I did. But what I am I going to do?"

"You pray and I'll pray," she said, "and we'll figure this out!"

I was amazed at her faith. Here I was, hoping she'd just tell me what to do, and she was asking me to rely solely on the Lord for help. Silently, I prayed again and asked Heavenly Father for guidance.

A few minutes later, I returned to the hair and make-up room. I walked back to the clothes rack and decided to look one more time to see if I could find a modest outfit. As I began to sift through the clothes, all of a sudden I saw an outfit hanging on the very end that I hadn't noticed before. Slowly I pulled it off the rack. My breath caught as I looked it up and down. It was a cap-sleeved V-neck shirt and knee-length skirt in exactly my size. It was blue, just like all the other outfits, but modest.

Heart pounding, I walked up to the same hair guy, outfit in hand, and asked if I could wear this one instead. He shrugged, and said, "If it fits."

It did, perfectly. That day I witnessed a small miracle. I know that prayers aren't always answered so quickly, but that day I gained a testimony of the power of prayer. I know that "whatsoever ye shall ask the Father in my name, which is right, believing that ye shall receive, behold it shall be given unto you." (3 Nephi 18:20).

As Bishop H. Burke Peterson once said, "Prayer strengthens faith. Prayer prepares us for the miracles of life. ("The Miracle of Prayer," *The Friend*, June 1974.)

Knowledge

Sometime during that first week after making the Top 12, we had an awesome opportunity to perform as a group at the Academy of Television Arts and Sciences. This was my first real taste of the "glam" life. After getting ready for the evening, we walked outside to see a huge, white stretch Excursion limo in the parking lot waiting to take us to our first red-carpet event. I had never even seen a "red carpet" before, and couldn't wait to actually walk down one for the first time.

As soon as we arrived and stepped out of the limo, cameras began to flash. I was told where to stand, and then suddenly the place erupted with, "Carmen, look over here! Right here, Carmen!" I didn't even have to fake a smile. I was pretty sure that the one I was wearing would be plastered to my face for the next year.

After our first group performance that night, we did a small press conference and then went outside to sign autographs. I hadn't really thought about what my signature should look like before then. But I did know that I didn't want to have to sign my first and last name every time—it would take too long. So I took the first paper that was handed to me, signed it "Carmen" and that was it.

It was a long yet exciting night, and to celebrate, we all went out to eat at a nice Italian restaurant. But some of the contestants decided to "celebrate" right then and there with some alcohol from the limo's mini bar. Pretty soon, everyone except Clay Aiken and I were drinking. Before coming out here, I couldn't have really told you what alcohol smelled like. Now, it was being passed around right in front of me.

"Hey, Carmen!" Corey Clark yelled from the back of the limo. "Could you pass us some?"

I looked down to see what he was talking about, and I saw that I was conveniently sitting by several bottles of alcohol. Reluctantly, I handed him one of the bottles, but as he grabbed it, some of it spilled onto my hand. I looked over in disgust at my grandma who was sitting next to me, and asked if she had a napkin so I could wipe it off.

"Hey, Carmen." I looked up to see Corey still staring at me. "I saw how you were eyeing that bottle when you passed it to me. It looked like you wanted to try some."

Now I had a choice to make. I could refuse to drink, or I

could try some—just a sip—to see what it was like. I knew my grandma wouldn't stop me. She might not agree with what I chose to do, but she would let me make my own decision.

Before I tell you what happened, let me share with you a quote from Elder Malcolm S. Jeppsen of the Seventy:

"Many of you will be, at some time or another, approached by one or more of your 'friends' who will entice you to do something you know you should not do—it might be something you know deep down inside will hurt you, your parents, and your Father in Heaven. It may be violating the Word of Wisdom or committing moral transgression, which is so displeasing to the Lord. 'No one will ever know,' the so-called 'friends' will tell you. 'Besides, what difference will it make?' My young friends, you don't have to reject your friends who are on the wrong path. You don't even have to give them up, necessarily. You can be their caring friend, ready to help them when they are ready to be helped. You can lift them and bear your testimony to them. Lead by example."

I was placed in a unique situation. I had not chosen to be in a limo with alcohol. I had not hand-picked these "friends." But I still could choose to drink or refuse.

Elder Jeppsen closes by saying, ". . . don't ever be led into displeasing your Father in Heaven by 'friends' who ask that as a condition of being your friend, you must choose between their way and the Lord's way. If that happens, choose the Lord's way. Then look for new friends.

"Above all, be a friend of the Savior. If you have not done so previously, now is the time to let him know you consider him your true friend and that you will be a true friend of his. With Jesus Christ as your friend, you will receive increased strength and testimony that will uphold you against temptations when they arise. That will without exception lift your vision and bring you comfort, guidance, peace, and other true friends.

"The Savior is the one friend who will always build you up, the one friend who is always true. Cultivate that friendship."

I took a deep breath, but before I could open my mouth, Clay piped up from the back seat, "No, Carmen's a Mormon. She wouldn't touch that stuff with a ten-foot pole!"

Immediately, Corey stopped pressuring me. I was *so grateful* to Clay for sticking up for me, even though I had never planned on taking that first drink. He respected my values. Clay was a true friend.

CHAPTER TEN

Standing in the Spotlight

"Her [religious guidelines] are restricting."
—Miles Siggons, wardrobe stylist
quoted in *Us* magazine

Before we knew it Tuesday night had rolled around and it was time for the competition to begin! The first week's theme was the music of Motown. I picked "You Can't Hurry Love" that was originally recorded by The Supremes and redone by the Dixie Chicks. I wanted to squeeze in as much country as I could!

While I was debating what to wear, my mom's friend from back home called to say that her nephew lived in Laguna Beach and had excellent taste, and that he and his friend would be thrilled to help me pick out modest clothes for TV. They were lifesavers! Because they also had the same standards that I did, I never worried that what they'd pick out would be immodest.

For this performance I wore a black frilly T-shirt and red capri pants with leopard flower heels. I felt very confident with my song, and performing it was actually FUN this time! I was still very nervous, but felt much more comfortable with my song, so I was able to relax a bit more onstage. Once again, after I finished I walked up to the dreaded "X" mark on the stage to receive the judges' comments.

Randy said, "You know what, I think that's the best I've ever heard you sing, dog."

Paula was super positive too (as usual) but it was Simon's comment that really made my night: "You justified my pick. Congratulations."

I ran backstage and Clay was waiting for me at the bottom of the stairs, and he gave me a huge hug. Everyone was giving me compliments and I think they were surprised at how different this performance was compared to the Wildcard show.

The format of the show was that we would perform on Tuesday night, and then the viewers across America would have two hours to vote for their favorite singer. Then on Wednesday night we would return for the "Results Show" where Ryan Seacrest would reveal which contestant had received the lowest number of votes, and would therefore be leaving the competition. This format would continue each week until that season's "American Idol" was named.

On Wednesday I learned that I was "safe" and would move on to the next round as part of the Top 11.

The next theme was Movie Hits—we could pick any song from a major motion picture. I selected "Hopelessly Devoted to You" from the musical *Grease*. I wore a beige top with a red necklace and a white skirt. I received positive comments from the judges and once again made it through, but the next day, I got several phone calls from friends and family commenting on how "bland" they thought my outfit was. I started to feel a little self-conscious, and the reality began to sink in that the entire country was watching me.

One day, I decided to go online and see what everyone was saying about me. Bad idea. I read some horrible things that some bloggers wrote on AmericanIdol.com—things like how my mom must've paid Simon to let me on the show, how I was the worst one, and how my vibrato made me sound like a goat. That comment hurt me the most. I used to love how my vibrato would kick in as soon as I stepped onstage. I admit, it did get a little crazy while I was on *Idol*, mostly due to nerves, but I didn't think I sounded like a farm animal!

I've always had a hard time with criticism. Which is really ironic, seeing that I had purposely tried out for a show that hosts the biggest critic in the world! (Simon.) But up until now, I'd never heard anything but positive feedback about my voice. I used to thrive on competition. I did my best under pressure, and I was always confident.

But now, because of the silly decision I made to read what other people thought of me, my way of thinking changed. I began to let their negative comments fester inside me until little by little, I started to believe them.

The theme for week three was Country Music, and it turned out to be tougher than I expected. It should have been a breeze for me, but instead of re-singing "Blue," the song that got me there, I chose to sing Martina McBride's "Wild Angels."

The song was a bit out of my range, and I was shaky that night. The judges weren't too rough on me. Simon even said I could replace the lead singer in the Dixie Chicks! But that was probably because they didn't want to crush me too hard. After all, Country night happened to fall on March 25—my birthday!

While auditioning for the show, the contestants all stayed in the La Meridian hotel. But once the first contestant left the show, the Top 11 moved into a mansion high atop the Hollywood Hills. We looked right down into Drew Barrymore's backyard!

We had a swimming pool, a hot tub, a work-out and game room, a private chef that came to prepare our meals, and an absolutely amazing view of L.A. I had it good the first couple of weeks—since I was under 18, I was required to have a parent or guardian stay with me at all times.

My dad, mom, grandma Darlene Rainey, and my sister Camille all took turns staying with me in the mansion. All of the girls upstairs had to share a room, but I had my own downstairs. It was sweet.

After I turned 18, though, it was "goodbye" to guardians (and three hours of school a day) and hello freedom! I moved upstairs with the other girls into the "master bedroom." We each had a teeny tiny single bed. There were four of us total, sharing a room, closet, and bathroom. It was chaotic, but so much fun!

It was my first taste of living on my own with roommates— it almost felt like a college dorm room. We'd stay up late talking and sharing secrets, listening to music, eating midnight snacks, and of course, practicing our upcoming songs.

Sometimes the other girls would go out on the town, and I'd be left alone. I brought along several *Harry Potter* books to read, and I would spend a lot of time in the evenings talking to my friends and family back home.

That week there was a huge article in the *Davis County Clipper* by Jan Hopkins about my 18th birthday. When my dad was asked in the article if my family was worried now that I was officially on my own, he responded, "Not really. Carmen's always had a good head on her shoulders. She's a good kid."

It went on to say, "He confesses he does worry about the things his daughter might be exposed to, and decisions she may have to make. But he's confident she has prepared herself well."

"She knows who she is," my grandma Darlene Rainey said. It's true that my family has constantly reminded me of who I am, what I stand for, and why it is imperative that I hold fast to the things I've been taught.

Something that helped me stay grounded was family prayer and scripture study every night over the phone. My mom said that sometimes she'd be in the kitchen cooking dinner and have a feeling that I needed her. So, she'd drop to her knees, right then and there, and pray for me. There were times that I literally felt strength beyond my own to face temptation, and I know it was because of all the prayers of my friends, family, and ward members.

No matter what exciting thing had happened during the day, no matter how many letters of fan mail I received, how many autographs I signed, I was still just Carmen at the end of the day, and my family constantly reminded me of who that Carmen was. They were so incredibly supportive—if it weren't for them, I would have been chewed up and spit out by the entertainment business.

One day I received two HUGE cards in the mail. One was from all my classmates in AP English, and the other was from all the girls in my ward's Young Women organization. Their words were so sweet and encouraging, especially since it was getting harder and harder for me to stay positive. I read those cards over and over, and I kept them in a box beside my bed to read when I was having a bad day.

I agree wholeheartedly with Marvin J. Ashton, former member of the Quorum of the Twelve Apostles when he said, "Encouragement can be quick and simple, but it is a voice of gladness that is needed by everyone." ("A Voice of Gladness," *Ensign*, May 1991.)

By this time, I had donned the nickname "little sister" and

all of the other contestants soon took it upon themselves to make sure "Baby Car-Car" didn't get corrupted while living in Hollywood.

They started doing this thing called "earmuffs." If one of them was about to swear or tell a dirty joke, they'd look at me and say, "Earmuffs, little sis!" And then it was my job, or the job of whomever was sitting closest to me, to cover my ears until they had finished talking. I loved being treated like the baby of the "family" and really grew to respect and look up to these new "older siblings."

Although we all came from different backgrounds, each of the *Idol* contestants believed in God and praying. The very first night we moved into the mansion, I was asked to say "grace" over the food. (It was almost like a re-enactment from the movie *Christmas Vacation:* "They want you to say grace—the blessing!")

As soon as I understood what they meant, I bowed my head and began to pray. No sooner had I said, "Dear Heavenly Father, we're so thankful for this food—" when I heard a loud "AMEN, LORD!" It startled me so much, I jerked my head up and looked around to see if everyone was okay. They all still had their eyes closed, waiting for me to go on. It was a very interesting (and loud!) prayer, but it somehow seemed to bring us closer together.

Before every performance, we would stand in a circle backstage, hold hands, and pray. Sometimes it would be me who offered it, sometimes it would be Clay or Kim or Ruben. All of us had different styles of praying, but we knew that however we did it, Heavenly Father would hear each and every one.

Our grueling week-to-week schedule was packed with Ford commercials, individual and group rehearsals, wardrobe shopping, recording studio visits to lay down our performance tracks, and endless interviews and photo shoots. So sometimes it was nice for us to just stop whatever we were doing and take a break. One night we decided to take our dinner downstairs and watch a movie together. I was the last one to dish up my food, and as I walked downstairs, I noticed that the movie had already started. As soon as I sat down with my plate of food, Rickey Smith leaned over and whispered, "Carmen, baby. This movie is rated R."

"Oh. Okay," I said, before picking up my plate to go back upstairs.

Suddenly, someone said, "Hey, Rickey, leave her alone. Her mom's not here—she's 18 now. She can stay if she wants."

Rickey responded, "But she says that Mormons don't watch R-rated movies, and I just thought she should know!"

"No, no, no, you're right, Rickey," I said. "I appreciate you telling me."

As I walked back upstairs to eat by myself, I thought how lonely it could be sometimes when you are doing what is right. Even though no one was around to stop me, I knew I'd feel unsettled if I stayed and watched that movie. It definitely wouldn't have made my life any better. I didn't lose the friendship of the other contestants because I had left the room, and I had a quiet peace settle over me after I walked away.

I have learned from experiences like this one that it is ALWAYS better for me to walk away, even if the movie isn't rated R. If it makes me feel uncomfortable for any reason, then I fast forward, change the channel, or turn it off. I've walked out of several movies in my lifetime, and have never looked back and regretted doing so. In fact, the only regrets I had were buying tickets for that movie in the first place!

For me, I have to be very sensitive to the small promptings from the Spirit, because they're not always persistent. It's usually,

"Carmen, you know you're not supposed to be doing this . . ." and then I'm left to make up my mind.

President Howard W. Hunter explains this perfectly when he said, "To fully understand this gift of agency and its inestimable worth, it is imperative that we understand that God's chief way of acting is by persuasion and patience and long-suffering, not by coercion and stark confrontation. He acts by gentle solicitation and by sweet enticement. He always acts with unfailing respect for the freedom and independence that we possess. He wants to help us and pleads for the chance to assist us, but he will not do so in violation of our agency. He loves us too much to do that, and doing so would run counter to his divine character."

I would encourage each one of you to learn to listen to and obey those quiet, loving promptings. As soon as you learn to recognize how the Spirit speaks to you, be sure to act on the advice and counsel that comes into your mind. Heavenly Father is a loving Father, and therefore will let us make mistakes based on our free agency. Know that He loves you NO MATTER WHAT! Show Him how much you love Him, too, by obeying His perfect counsel. It's always easier in the long run.

Divine Nature

Something interesting happened during week four of the competition. This was my favorite week—Disco! I sang Jennifer Lopez's version of "Turn the Beat Around." I was waiting around in the hair and make-up room to get ready when I saw Dean Banowitz, the hairstylist, putting extensions in Julia DeMato's hair.

I asked him if he could put some in for me, too, and he said yes! I had never, ever had hair past my shoulders, so it was such a fun change for me. In fact, in *Us* magazine the following week I had a half-page about me that said, "New and Improved: Teen Queen Carmen! Her Hot New Look."

The article talked about my new hair style, how Simon "digged" my "sleek new extensions" because he dubbed me the most "commercial" of the contestants that night.

Then the *Us* article proceeded to comment on my wardrobe: "Clothes-wise, Rasmusen is less free to experiment. The Bountiful Utah resident's Mormon 'church [request] she not show too much leg, midriff' or cleavage, says Siggens. Plus, Rasmusen's mom must approve all outfits."

The article added, "'She has a fantastic figure,' says Siggens, 'so [her religious guidelines] are restricting.'"

I always thought that that line was so funny: "Her religious guidelines are restricting!" The world thinks that the standards and values the Church has set are restricting. But they are *so wrong*! Our guidelines give us freedom—freedom from sin, sorrow, and guilt. Freedom from Satan's grasp.

By now, everyone knew that I was a Mormon, and I started getting a lot of questions from other contestants about why the Church had so many "rules." I would get some hard questions that I didn't always know how to answer. My seminary teacher back home must've been inspired, because one day I received a box that had about 30 *For the Strength of Youth* packets and 23 pass-along cards stacked inside.

I began to hand them out, and so when one of the contestants would ask me why I didn't wear mini-skirts I'd say, "Well, if you turn to this page of your *For the Strength of Youth* packet, you can read about modesty." Those packets were a blessing! I wish I would've carried one with me at all times while I was in high school. Even knowing you have the packet with you can sometimes be enough to steer you away from temptation.

I love what Sister Julie B. Beck, now President of the General Relief Society, said when she was serving as First Counselor of the Young Women's organization: "If you're unapologetic about blessings, then you can't be apologetic about what gets you the blessings."

It takes a lot of courage to do what's right—but you can do it!

As Elder Jeffrey R. Holland of the Twelve said, "Be a woman of Christ. Cherish your esteemed place in the sight of God. He needs you. This Church needs you. The world needs you." ("To Young Women," *Ensign*, Nov 2005, 28)

CHAPTER ELEVEN

Heading Down the Homestretch

"Carmen was the glue that held everyone together."
—Paula Abdul, after I was voted off the show

The theme for week five was Billboard No. 1 Hits. I had a hard time picking a song this week. I sat in the *American Idol* office for hours listening to songs on Susan Slammer's computer. Finally, I settled on Blondie's "Call Me." I have to admit that I had no idea what Deborah Harry, the lead singer of Blondie, was talking about when she sang "Call Me." I just thought it was a cute, up-tempo song and would work well with my voice. (And, I thought it was a cute play on words—I wanted voters to "Call [in for] Me!")

I wore a jean jacket and an army skirt with high top black boots. I felt pretty good about it, but in rehearsal, the judges all looked at me like I was crazy.

I remember Patrick (the very first guy I auditioned in front of) walking with me around the building, trying to help me calm down. Apparently, everyone thought I sounded terrible, and knowing that didn't help my confidence at all.

By the time the show started, I was a nervous wreck. When I finished singing my song, Paula said, "Carmen, you're a doll. You're adorable. This is bad-girl kind of song."

Simon told me it was "just a wrong choice of song" and proclaimed it "absolutely dreadful." I walked off stage that night totally confused.

Later, my singing teacher called me to say he talked to one of his friends in California who also happened to be a vocal coach, and said they both thought it was one of my best performances to date. But everyone on the show (including the vocal coach, Byrd) thought it was awful. I couldn't figure out who was telling the truth. I was inclined to trust my singing teacher, Dean, but why would everyone else tell me something completely different?

The worst one to figure out was Randy. He'd give me his classic "It was pitchy dog," and "I don't know, I just wasn't really feeling it," and then when I'd see him in halls after the show and ask him what I could work on, he'd say, "Nothin', dog! You da bomb! You're doin' great!"

Suddenly I felt like I couldn't trust anyone—like everyone was trying to play mind games with me to psych me out. And unfortunately, it was working.

I can honestly say, I've never had it so hard. I would be backstage, shaking, and freezing and sweating and just completely beside myself because I was so afraid that I wouldn't perform well and that no one would like me. I'd step out on the stage without the sparkle and pizazz I usually had. I just wanted to go out there and get it over with.

All growing up, I didn't really have to practice too much to pull something off. I just did it. Everything in my life had always come easy to me. I had never had dance lessons and made the Starz team when I was 9. I always had solos in my singing groups, made the prestigious singing group called Onstage, faked my way through tough dance and cheer routines in high school, was vice president of my Dance Company, and won 1st or 2nd place in all the county and state fair talent competitions. So when I was competing on *American Idol,* I thought it would be the same. Get up there, look pretty, wow everyone with my stage presence and battta bing batta boom, I'd sail right through the competition. But it was turning out to be much harder than I thought.

Week six was the week that killed me. By now, my confidence was shredding. I had no idea what to expect from the judges, what would impress the viewers, and most importantly, how to keep my voice steady on stage. Every week I seemed to get more and more shaky, and I was constantly frustrated when I'd watch my performances back, thinking, "That's not how I really sound! Aaah!"

And this week was by far the worst. I had no idea what song to sing for this week's theme, which was songs by Billy Joel. In fact, Clay picked the one song I would've felt comfortable with, "Tell Her About It." And no way was I competing with Clay!

I couldn't make up my mind, and finally just settled on "And So It Goes," because I remembered our high school choir singing it at one point. I wasn't crazy about the song, and I wasn't crazy about my outfit, either.

I had chosen to wear a blue and green tie-dyed silk dress with a jean jacket. But there was a problem: the jean jacket didn't fit properly, and unfortunately I waited until the DAY OF THE SHOW to figure that out.

As I showed the stylists my problem, they said, "Well, just wear the dress as it is."

But the dress was a tube top. I refused, and they got frustrated with me. I stood my ground, and finally ended up wearing my black T-shirt I had on underneath the dress. In a last attempt to rescue the outfit, the stylists pinned on several colorful buttons and tied a blue leather ribbon around my neck before I went on stage, going for "funky." But instead, I ended up looking like a dressed up poodle posing as a mermaid.

What made things even worse, was that this was the week my friends had chosen to drive out to see me! I wanted to die when I walked out on stage and saw their eyebrows shoot up and their eyes grow wide as they saw what I was wearing. I don't think I smiled the entire song.

Because I seriously lacked confidence (and style) I performed poorly that night. Simon told me that I sounded like a child singing at a birthday party, and if "I were the mother of that child, I'd say. 'Shut up!'" Not exactly the confidence booster I was hoping for. As we went to a commercial break, Ryan Seacrest whispered in my ear, "Don't worry. We'll get you the votes you need."

I slumped off the stage in my hideous outfit, ready to ball my eyes out when I saw Kim Caldwell standing at the top of the stairs with her arms outstretched, waiting for me. She had received negative comments too, and yet here she was wanting to comfort me. I ran into her arms and began to sob.

"Don't worry, babe," she said. "It's just Blonde Bashing night."

The next night Kim and I were both in the bottom three—and she ended up getting the boot. I was so sad. Kim had protected me and looked out for me the entire time I was on the show, and I didn't want to see her leave.

My singing teacher, Dean, seeing my serious drop in confidence as I stood there in the bottom three that week, decided to pack up his family and come out to L.A. for moral support and to help me get my voice back in shape. Up until this point, I'd been warming up with him over the phone, but he felt it crucial to have good face-to-face positive interaction.

The upcoming week's theme was songs written by Diane Warren. He helped me pick the song, "Love Will Lead You Back." I practiced for hours and hours in a little studio in downtown L.A. where apparently Michael Jackson and Celine Dion had once practiced in, too.

Little by little, all the layers of fear and inadequacy began to melt away until I felt confident again with my voice. I performed for Dean's family over and over again until finally Dean said, "That's enough! We're taking you out tonight, Carmen. You need to take your mind off of things and have a night of fun."

We all drove down to the Santa Monica Pier and rode the roller coaster, bought junk food, and didn't talk about my upcoming performance once. It was very therapeutic for me, and I have to admit, probably did more for my self-esteem than anything else. That night, I felt like Carmen again.

When Tuesday finally rolled around, I was much more confident than I had been the week before. I sang my heart out, despite my nerves. But despite my best effort, it still wasn't as good as it was when I had been practicing it for Dean's family. I knew right then and there that I was not going to move on. And then Randy made his meanest comment yet: "You know dog, we're looking for the number one singer in America, and I don't think you're even close, dog."

I felt my heart sink. Oooo, how I disliked Randy Jackson at that moment! I swore, if he said "dog" one more time, I was going to leap off the stage and beat him with my microphone stand. (My mom later confessed that she also had angry feelings towards Randy—she said she wished she would've given me a squirt gun so I could spray him in the face with cold water and say "Cool it!" whenever he gave me a nasty comment!)

Paula said that although it wasn't her favorite, I could be proud of myself because I came back from last week stronger and more confident. Simon agreed with both, and then said, "Well, you can't win this competition. You can't!"

As I walked over to sit by Ryan, he asked me if I thought that I could win the competition.

"I absolutely think I have a shot at winning this competition," I told him. "It's about coming back and being better, and that's exactly what I've done tonight." It was a complete lie. I may have done better, but I knew in my heart that I wouldn't go on. This was my last week on *Idol*.

I had always believed in myself, before *American Idol*. I just knew that no matter how hard everyone said it was to try and become a singer, that I would do it. I would make it. Period! I think that determination is what got me on the show. I believed I was meant to be on it, and so everyone else did, too. My mom always used to tell me, "Fake it till you make it!"

When I was 9, my grandpa filmed me singing in my front room. I don't remember exactly why we did that. I think my mom thought that if she could just show people how talented I was, that someone would for sure want to make me a star. In truth, that home movie was hilarious. It's one of those things I played for my husband before we were married to say, "See how big of a geek I was?"

When I was 12, I remember going to the grocery store with my mom, and the K-Bull 93 guys were out front broadcasting live. She marched right up to them and said, "You've got to hear her sing. Sing them something, Carmen." So I did. They were impressed, and told us to come down to the studio one day and they'd put me on the air. A few days later, we drove down at about six a.m. and I sang "No One Needs to Know" and dedicated it to my dad for his birthday. They played about 15 seconds of it. Then, I sang "Blue" off air, and I remember one the DJs tearing down a picture of LeAnn Rimes and saying, "Forget her! You're just as good!"

And I believed I was. I remember thinking to myself one day, "What would be the most horrible thing that anyone could ever take away from me?" Without hesitation, I thought, "My voice." The thing that I loved most about myself was my voice. Now, it was one of the things I liked least. I guess it just shows what so much negativity can do to a person's mind and attitude and way of thinking.

The next night, I promised myself that I wouldn't cry when I heard the results. I knew I was going home. But even still, when Ryan announced that I would be leaving the competition and my "good-bye video" started to play, I couldn't help the tears from coming. It had been such an amazing ride, such a wonderful experience . . . and now it was over.

As I walked backstage after the show to say good-bye to everyone, each of the judges congratulated me on making it so far. I loved Paula's comment to my mom, "Carmen was the glue that held everyone together."

I'm sure I got a few, "Yo, yo, dog!" and "You da bomb! You da bomb! Yea, yea, yea!" comments from Randy, but it was Simon's last comment to me that really meant the most. He said, "You have really tough skin, and I really respect you for that."

It was all kind of surreal to me, leaving the show. My parents came back to the house with me that night to help me box up all my stuff. It felt weird knowing this would be last time I'd share a room with the other girls. The mansion had become strangely quiet now that there were only six of us left—now soon to be five.

The next morning dawned bright and early, and before I

knew what was really happening, I was traveling on a plane to New York City to do follow-up interviews on the *Today* show, MTV's *TRL*, *Inside Edition*, *Entertainment Tonight*, *E!*, and, best of all, *David Letterman*. I didn't exactly get to do an interview with him. Instead, I read the "Top Ten Reasons Why You Won't Win *American Idol*." It was by far the coolest thing I've done to date!

After getting booted from the show, I thought I'd have a couple of weeks to settle down and relax before tour started. Not so. I was flown back to L.A. every week for guest performances, and finale rehearsals. It was so fun to get everyone together again.

The finale was a ball, and I even had my own private limo for the night! My family all came out and had a ball riding around with me to autograph signings and parties. I was really surprised to see how many people really liked me after all.

I stood for more than an hour signing autographs. One boy was so excited to see me that he threw his arms around me and squeezed me so tightly that I almost couldn't breathe. The security guard had to pry him off of me—it was kind of scary!

The whole thing left me absolutely exhausted, and the crazy thing was, it wasn't over just yet—we still had the *American Idols Live!* tour to look forward to.

Soon after the finale, I received a letter from six-year-old Kirsten Tymchuck of New York. She sent me a little book, complete with pictures she drew herself and the story that concludes this chapter.

At the end of the book, she drew a picture of herself with big blue teardrops falling all the way to the floor. I cried when I read it, too!

"The Camin Story"
by Kirsten Tymchuck

"Tonight my favit person got kick
off of American Idol. This is my story of how it happind.
First, Josh, Trenyce and Camin were in the bottom three.
Then Ryan said, "Do yoo think that everybody should be here?"
Then when the judges told the people the stuff, they sent
Trenyce back to safety ("Yes!")
Then it was just Josh and Camin in the bottom three, and Josh
got back to safety ("Yes!")
Then Camin did a last song for us . . .
And I stardid to cry.
The End"

CHAPTER TWELVE

48 Cities in 65 Days

*"Carmen, we've made a decision. We've decided
that we want to raise our daughters Mormon!"*
—Fellow *Idol* finalists Julia DeMato
and Kimberly Caldwell

Coming home was weird. Having everyone recognize me everywhere I went was even weirder.

FOX teamed up with the radio station 97.1 ZHT and threw me a "Welcome Home!" party at the SkyBox restaurant in downtown Salt Lake. On my way in, a group of girls noticed me and started screaming.

"Oh my gosh! It's Carmen Rasmusen! Can we please have your autograph?"

I don't think any of us contestants really realized how huge the show was, how many people had seen and voted for us on TV, and it still surprised me that people wanted my autograph. We were living in a bubble the whole time we were on the show and it was like that bubble had suddenly popped and we were left on our own. It was like I had been put in a time machine, because everything and everyone was different when I got home.

All of my friends had these new inside jokes, and I started to feel like an outsider. I had gone through so much in the last year that they just didn't understand or relate to, and vice versa. My group of friends that I had so loved being with through the ups and downs of high school had all grown so close in my absence. While I still felt like they considered me their friend, it seemed like the invisible rope that had once bound us together so tightly had begun to fray.

The day of high school graduation was a blur. I was so ready to get out of school and start my own "career." But it also was a little sad to look around at my classmates and realize I might not see some of them for a long time.

Fellow *Idol* contestant Kimberley Locke flew out to be with me on my special day, and she gave me a silver music box as a graduation present with "CARMEN, THE BEST IS YET TO COME" engraved on the lid. She was right.

I was only given the luxury of relaxing for about a month before I would begin rehearsals for the *American Idols Live!* tour. When I was voted off the show, I felt so sad to be leaving everyone. We had truly become like one big dysfunctional family. But now we'd be together again non-stop for the next two months.

I flew out to St. Paul, Minnesota at the end of June. It was so much fun learning all the dances and new songs for the tour! I was grateful that the judges wouldn't be coming along with us this time—although to my dismay, Randy Jackson did make a surprise appearance a week before our first show to see how everything was turning out!

During one of the rehearsals, Julia DeMato and Kimberly Caldwell came up to me and said, "Carmen, we've made a decision. We've decided that we want to raise our daughters Mormon!" Shocked, I asked them why they had decided that. "Well, we want them to turn out like you."

I was so touched. Here were two girls from very different walks of life, and who had very different standards than I did, yet they could see the benefit of living a gospel-centered life. They respected my values and standards so much that they wanted their children to have the same kind of life I had growing up.

Until that point, I didn't realize how observant people were of my lifestyle. Like it or not, because I was in the "spotlight" people were looking to me as an example and role model for The Church of Jesus Christ of Latter-day Saints.

I should have been terrified at having such a huge responsibility placed on my shoulders—and at times I was. But I had been taught true, eternal principles that guided my actions and decisions and helped me remain strong in the worst of situations.

Elder Richard G. Scott of the Quorum of the Twelve said, "I commend each one of you select young men and women who live a righteous life, who consistently make decisions based upon eternal truths and not upon that which seems to be most appealing at the moment. In doing right you enlist the help of God to sustain you to be victorious. You need not fear the future. For you, it will be glorious as you continue to obey the laws of God." (*Ensign*, Nov. 1998, p. 68)

The scriptures have amazing examples of real-life people who lived long ago, yet overcame temptations by relying on the Lord and "denying themselves of all ungodliness" (Moroni 10:32) because they learned for themselves that "wickedness never was happiness." (Alma 41:10).

I have always worn a CTR ring. In high school, it was the pinkie ring that Camille gave me, and after *Idol*, it was one I received from a boy I was dating. It had a little crystal below the "CTR" and I guess sort of looked like a class ring to non-members. Some of the contestants commented on it, and asked what the "T" stood for. Confused, I asked them what they meant.

They said, "Like, Carmen Rasmusen . . . but what's your middle name? What does the 'T' stand for?"

"Oh!" I laughed. "This ring doesn't stand for my initials. It actually stands for Choose The Right!"

Another time, I was writing a letter to this same guy who gave me the ring who had now left on a mission. Clay came up to me and pretended to read the letter over my shoulder.

"Hey!" I threw my arms over the paper, trying to cover it.

"Oh, Carmen, don't worry," Clay said. "I'm not going to read what you're writing to your priest."

My priest? I guess because it said "Elder" on it, Clay thought I was writing a letter of confession!

The day of our first *American Idols Live!* show was fab-u-lous! We had two huge tour buses—I was on the bus with Ruben, Clay and Kimberley Locke. I slept on the very top bunk—er, relaxed is more like it. By the time we got on the bus after the shows each night, it was close to 11:00 p.m. Naturally, we were all starving after having expended so much energy on stage, and so we'd usually have a very late supper. We would drive for about five hours or longer toward our next destination, and then we would file off the buses to check into the hotels around 4:00 a.m.

That was the only time I really got to sleep—in the hotel room, by myself. Around noon I would wake up and get ready in order to be back on the bus by 2:00 p.m. Then we would drive to the next arena, do interviews, eat an early dinner, and then head into the hair and make-up room to get ready for that night's show. It was a strange routine, but I got used to it.

I loved hearing the crowd go wild as soon as the lights went down. It was a three-hour show. During the first half, all of us would sing solo numbers, and during the second half we performed together on a medley of songs. We sold out a lot of shows, and it felt so great to get up there and just have a ball without worrying about being on TV or having judges commenting on our performances.

However, I soon discovered that even then I wasn't fully immune to criticism—I had several bad reviews in local newspapers along the way. One day, we all sat down for breakfast and a camera crew was there with a newspaper review in hand. They gave the copy to Clay and wanted him to read it out loud so they could get our reactions on film. It was such a cruel and twisted thing to do, and while I don't remember exactly what was said about me, I do know that it was very negative and stuck with me for several weeks.

Integrity

Sometimes we would watch movies on the bus. I usually had to fight to get the TV first, or chances were that the others would want to watch an R-rated movie. I used to just sit up in my tiny little bunk alone, wishing I had something to do.

One day, I received a HUGE bag of DVDs from some fans—they were an answer to prayer! Because I made a decision not to watch the R movies with the other contestants, I was blessed with lots and lots of my own. I borrowed the tour manager's laptop, and would look forward to crawling up in my bunk and watching the DVDs.

Some of the guys on the bus used to bring dirty magazines on with them. But a lot of them "strangely disappeared." I wonder how that happened? You can bet I had a hand in throwing out every disgusting magazine I came across! Pretty soon, they caught on and either hid them from me or stopped buying them.

One day, there were about five of us all seated in the back of the bus talking. Suddenly the tour manager looked over at me and said, "Carmen, would you pose for Playboy for $100,000?"

I didn't even hesitate. "No way."

"How about $500,000? Would you do it for $500.000?"

"Nope."

"Okay, a million dollars. You can't tell me you'd turn down one million dollars!"

I looked him squarely in the eye. "My integrity is worth so much more than that—I wouldn't lower my standards for any amount of money."

After a month or so on the tour, I was tired of the whole music business scene. I was tired of getting criticized. I was tired of being in the shadows of Clay and Ruben and Kim Locke. I was ready to move on with my life, and I wanted to go home.

Before I went on stage one night toward the end of the tour, one of the security guards handed me a book that a fan had left for me. It was filled with positive, uplifting comments from people who were fans of mine, and pictures of me performing on the show. It was exactly what I needed to keep me going for just for a little bit longer.

Finally the tour reached my hometown: Salt Lake City! I will never, ever forget how crazy the crowd went as soon as they announced that I would be the next performer.

When I was in junior high, I went to a Dixie Chicks concert at the Delta Center with my best friend, Corrine. I remember Natalie Maines saying, "Never give up on your dreams!" Every night after that, I'd lay in bed and imagine performing on the Delta Center stage in front of thousands of people, all screaming and clapping for me. Now, suddenly that dream had come true. As I walked out on stage that night, the crowd erupted. It was so loud that I couldn't even hear myself sing! It was the greatest feeling in the world. All of my friends and family came back to see me after the show. They wished me luck in the following weeks as the tour headed toward its conclusion.

One day as we were eating dinner before a show, Kim and Julia came into the dressing room and announced that the cooks had made their favorite dessert—tiramasu. I had never heard of it before, and asked what it was like.

"Oh, it's soooooo good!" they gushed. "It has yummy chocolatey layers and cream and has fine crumbles of espresso coffee in it!" Coffee? No thanks.

"Don't worry, Carmen," they said, guessing what I was thinking. "It's just a teeny, tiny bit. And sometimes they leave the coffee out. You have to try some!" Each girl had a separate piece in their hands, and were making "mmm, mmm" sounds as they ate.

I thought about it for awhile, and decided to talk to the cooks about how they prepared it, just to be safe. "Oh, we don't make ours with any coffee," the cooks responded when I asked them. Whew! I reached for a piece just as they were saying, "Instead, we soak it in rum!"

Boo. Rum means alcohol. "But most of it gets all cooked out, so don't worry. You won't get drunk or anything!"

I wasn't worried about getting drunk, but I was worried about eating the tiramasu, even if the cooks said the alcohol did get cooked out. Cake in hand, I wandered back into the dressing room where everyone else was waiting. "Oh, good, you got a piece!"

"Yeah, but I don't know if I should eat it." I looked at the cake, going back in forth in my head about what I should do.

"Eat it," Julia started. "Eat it!" Kim Caldwell joined in. Pretty soon, everyone was chanting, "EAT IT! EAT IT! EAT IT!"

I couldn't believe what was happening. Talk about peer pressure! I remember looking at my plate, desperately trying to make a decision when I heard a faint *"Caaarrmeeen . . ."* coming from down the hall.

"CARMEN! NOOOOOO!" The voice was getting louder, and just as I was lifting the fork to my mouth, Joe, one of our tour managers, came barreling into the room.

"Carmen! You can't eat that!" He was panting, completely out of breath. "It's . . . soaked in . . . rum!"

I was shocked that Joe had run all the way down the hall in a panic just to tell me that. All of the others rolled their eyes, but I seriously wanted to cry. How could I possibly eat it now? Whether or not the alcohol was cooked out, Joe understood that I did not drink *or* eat alcohol, so he did his best to protect me from doing so. I will never forget how he defended himself as everyone made fun of him for coming to my "rescue."

"I just thought she should know!" he exclaimed.

People are always going to be watching us, and believe it or not—they actually want us to stay true to our values! Even if they don't personally agree with our way of living, they still know the difference between right and wrong.

I very much respected Joe for coming to my rescue and wanting to protect my innocence.

Taken during the first photo shoot of the Top 12 finalists. Clockwise from left, Vanessa Olivarez, Corey Clark, Charles Grigsby, me, Trenyce, Ruben Studdard, Clay Aiken, Kimberly Locke, Julia DeMato, Josh Gracin, Kimberly Caldwell, and Rickey Smith.

This was the day of the "blue" shoot. I'm wearing the outfit that I found on the clothes rack as an answer to my prayers.

During my time on American Idol, my high school showed its full support, as demonstrated by this sign outside the school.

With my grandma Darlene Rainey, who often spent time with me in Los Angeles during the competition.

Mom snapped this photo of me with American Idol judges Simon Cowell and Randy Jackson.

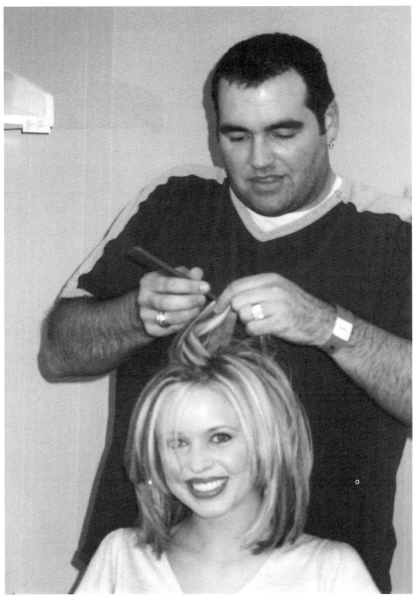

The daily routine of getting my hair and make-up done was time-consuming, but we had some of the top people in the industry helping us look our best..

The day after I was voted off American Idol, I suddenly found myself on my way to New York City to do a series of media appearances. Here I am with TV entertainment correspondent Billy Bush.

Two of my best friends on the show, fellow American Idol contestants Julia DeMato and Kimberly Caldwell.

When I returned home to Bountiful, Utah, after the competition, FOX reporter Lane Lyon interviewed me during a party that my family and friends had organized.

Graduation day! Kim Locke flew out to help me celebrate.

On stage with Julia and Kim during the American Idols Live! tour.

During the tour I performed several solo numbers. It was a dream come true to be on stage in the Delta Center in front of friends and family.

CHAPTER THIRTEEN

Stadium of Fire

"Wednesday was a BLAST! Brad and I hiked up to these awesome waterfalls by Mt. Timpanogos. We (well, I) made a lunch and we had a picnic up there. I found out a lot of stuff about him that I liked."

—My July 18, 2004 journal entry at age 19

Well, before we knew it, tour had come to a close. We had been to 48 cities in 65 days and were totally and completely worn out. I, for one, decided to take a break from the whole music scene and planned on heading down to Provo to attend Brigham Young University in the fall—actually, more like the day after I got home from tour! I needed time to breathe, time to rejuvenate, and time to figure out who I was and what I wanted to do for the rest of my life.

My sister and brother-in-law signed me up for all my classes, bought all my books, and my parents helped me move in the day before the semester started. It may seem a bit overwhelming for some to go from a national tour to a university so soon, but for me, it was just what the doctor ordered.

Because I wasn't able to go to church that much while I was on *Idol* and on tour due to rehearsals and performances, my sister thought it was extremely important that I refill my "spirituality tank." Almost all of my classes that first semester were church-related classes: Marriage Prep, Family Life, Book of Mormon, Teachings of the Living Prophets, and Sharing the Gospel were all on my schedule.

I can't tell you how much happier I was now that I was attending BYU. It just felt right. I had so much fun living in the dorms and making new friends, and again being in an atmosphere where I was around others who had the same beliefs that I did. But I was still in the "diva" mode a little bit.

The first day of school I wore a bright orange shirt with funky writing all over it, and orange fringe hanging off the sides. I put a huge orange flower in my hair, and wore stitched-up colored jeans and suede pointy boots. (I guess when the judges first said, "Welcome to Hollywood!" I really took it to heart!) I looked ridiculous. It took me awhile to catch on to the "college look"—for so long, I'd been sporting over-the-top performing outfits.

Because I was suddenly the new "celebrity" attending the Y, I was asked to perform—a lot. I hated it. My confidence level was shot from being on *American Idol.* I honestly had no desire whatsoever to sing, ever again.

I didn't want to be a county singer anymore. I couldn't get up on stage without imagining everyone judging me. I just wanted to live a normal college life, and get away from the whole entertainment business (although I did try my hand in acting in the local LDS film *Pride and Prejudice*).

One night I decided to go for a hike up to Y Mountain with a guy I was dating. It was a pretty hard hike, and when we got to the top, we spread out a blanket, pulled out the little DVD player we had brought up with us, and settled down to watch the movie *Charlie*.

There was a group of people that were sitting next to us, and all of a sudden, one of the girls in the group said, "Hey, have any of you guys seen *Pride and Prejudice*?" I stiffened. "What in the world is Carmen Rasmusen doing in that film, anyway? I mean, we all know she can't sing!"

I couldn't believe it. Here I was, sitting atop a mountain for crying out loud, and I still couldn't escape the nasty criticism! I wanted to march right over to that girl and give her piece of my mind. Instead, I just put my head in my hands and cried and cried.

All my life, the only thing I ever wanted to be was a singer. In fourth grade, we had a career day. We had a huge assembly where various men and women came to speak to us on setting goals for the future. I already knew what I wanted to do. I remember one of the ladies saying, "Now, some of you might want to be pro athletes, or famous movie stars, or singers. But the odds are that only about 1 in about every 100,000 make things like that. Now, we're not telling you to give up on your dreams—but have a backup plan."

I didn't have a backup plan. I didn't need a backup plan. I would make it, even if I died trying. I wouldn't, I couldn't do anything else. I always knew what I wanted. I remember looking at my friends' papers, and they had three or four options written down. I wrote only one: Country Singer. Now, that goal seemed a million miles away.

I came home for the Christmas holidays, and one day a man came to the door, asking for me. Turns out, he was in my parents ward. His name was Greg Ericksen, and he was the husband of one of my old YW leaders. He said that he'd heard me sing, and wanted to be my manager. He said that he believed in me, and thought I had what it took to go all the way. I admit I was a little wary at first, but decided to give it a try, anyway. Little by little, my confidence started coming back. I went into the recording studio to lay down demo tracks. Every time I'd mess up, Greg would just say, "It's okay. You're doing great!" It was a 180-degree turn from the criticism I was used to. I actually felt good when I left the recording studio—something I hadn't felt for a long, long time.

Pretty soon, we were flying out to L.A. to pitch the songs to major pop record labels. But something didn't feel right— I wasn't a pop singer, I was a country singer. I had a long talk with my manager about this one night, and asked if I could try my hand at writing a country song, and then go to Nashville. He told me to go for it.

I remember sitting in the tiny piano room in the basement of my dorm and writing a song called "Photograph." My manager ended up liking it so much that a few weeks later, we were on our way to Nashville!

I was still very naive when it came to the whole music business thing. I thought that it would take me one, maybe two years max to get signed to a major recording deal because of the exposure I had when I was on *Idol*. I performed for every major label in town, worked with several different songwriters, knocked on a ton of different doors, and always got the same response: "We're just not interested right now." I couldn't believe it.

Josh Gracin, who was also on my season, had come to Nashville several months before and got signed with Lyric Street Records, the same label that signed SheDaisy and Rascal Flatts. I couldn't understand why he could get a record deal, and I couldn't. But I didn't give up. I did showcase after showcase, trying to show them my "dedication." It was hard to hear, "So, when are you moving to Nashville?"

I was to told to say "Oh, soon!"—even though I didn't know for sure if it would ever happen. Suddenly, it was like I was playing all these little games with everyone, and I felt like I was being judged all over again.

After about a year and still no record deal, my manager and I decided to record a four-song EP to let the fans know that I was still here, making music. We released "Photograph" independently, and got great reviews from independent promoters and charts. I even won "Best New Country Artist of the Year" at the New Music Weekly awards show in L.A., and "Photograph" shot to the Top Ten on iTunes within 24 hours. I finally thought I was on my way.

In the summer of 2004, I was asked to perform for the Stadium of Fire for the Freedom Festival with several other reality show contestants. Reba McEntire was the headliner that year, and we were the opening and closing acts. It was a blast! 65,000 thousand people packed the LaVell Edwards Stadium in Provo—one of the biggest crowds I'd ever performed in front of. Little did I know that somewhere among all those people in the stadium that day, my future husband was waiting!

Bradley Paul Herbert was serving a mission in Puerto Rico while I was on *American Idol*, and had never seen nor heard of me. In fact, he thought I was some girl from Nashville just in town for the this event. He heard my name for the first time over the loud speaker, and started joking around with his brother-in-law about how cool it would be to somehow get my attention and then ask me out on a date. And then, as fate would have it, the opportunity presented itself.

After I finished singing, I sat down on the lawn by the other performers—just a few rows in front of him. And, he realized that the girl sitting next to me was Jody—a friend of one of his sisters! Brad decided to tap a little boy on the shoulder sitting on the last row of the lawn in front of him, and asked him if he would get the girl sitting next to "the curly blonde" to come back and talk to him. (Determination has never been a lacking quality for Brad—if he wants something, he'll find a way to get it!)

All of a sudden, Jody left. A few minutes later she came back, and leaned over to me.

"Hey! There's this boy back there who wants to meet you! He's sitting right behind us with his family, and his dad's running for Lt. Governor right now!"

"WHAT?!" It was so loud, and we were sitting right by the speakers. I couldn't really understand what she was saying.

"JUST COME BACK HERE AND MEET HIM!"

Grabbing her hand, I followed her back to where the first row of bleachers started and looked up to see a very handsome family smiling back at me. Meanwhile Brad, apparently in shock that he had gotten this far, began rummaging around for a pen while I went down the row, shaking first his mom then his dad's hands, and then each of his brothers and sisters, wondering which one wanted to meet me.

Finally, I got to the very end of the row and saw a brown-haired boy wearing a button-up collared shirt. He locked eyes with me and said, "Hey! I'm Brad. Can I have your autograph?" I quickly took the program, signed it, and handed it back. Jody was still talking to Brad's dad, and asked if there were any conventions coming up that she could sing at. He gave her a card, and she wrote her number on the back. Nudging me, she asked what my number was. I told her, and stole another glance at this Brad kid. I decided he was pretty cute. As Jody handed the card back to his dad, I silently wished that Brad would catch on and realize that my number was really meant for him, not his dad. Smart boy—he did!

The next day, I saw Brad's mom at the Marriott Center where I sang the National Anthem. I was actually with another boy (we'll call him Melvin), that I wasn't too crazy about. Luckily, my mom and grandma were with me, and did me a favor by distracting Melvin while I hurried up to the front to find Brad's mom, just as she was coming over to say hi to me! We got to talking, and all of a sudden I blurted, "Hey, have your son call me!"

"Really? Aren't you . . . dating someone?" She glanced over at Melvin, who was politely trying to break away from my grandma's surprisingly firm grasp.

"Oh, no! He's just a friend. Seriously, have your son call me!" Looking back, that was a pretty bold thing for me to do! I had never asked the mother of a boy I had a crush on to have her son call me! She told me she'd tell him, and began to talk to me about how wonderful he was, and how he had such an amazing sense of humor and positive outlook on life. She said he was the life of the family, the "golden child." (And she wasn't kidding!)

Sure enough, about a week later, I got a message on my phone.

"Hey, Carmen, I don't know if you remember me, but this is Brad. You met me at the Stadium of Fire. . ." I was so excited to hear from him, I screamed. I immediately called him back, but got his machine as well. He tried texting me back the next night, but I had already fallen asleep. Finally, on Friday morning, he called again. He asked me if I wanted to go to a LeAnn Rimes concert down at the Thanksgiving Point waterfall amphitheater—that night! Of course I said yes, and immediately began getting ready for the evening.

I still remember Brad's face as I yelled down, "Just a minute!" as I finished up getting ready. He looked up to me with an expression of what looked like a mix of hope, anxiety, and anticipation. After all, this was basically a blind date we had set up ourselves! I remember thinking that he looked different from what I remembered—and, on closer look, I noticed he had braces.

On the way down, I decided that no matter what, I would just let loose and have fun tonight. It turned out to be the best first date I'd ever been on. I laughed so hard my sides hurt. Brad was confident, funny, caring, and by far the nicest guy I'd ever met. He didn't even care that I had huge sweat rings underneath my arms because of a) the heat, and b) duh, I sweat when I'm nervous! (I felt a little better when his "invisible" clear braces became a quite visible shade of pink after eating a red sno-cone.) Pretty soon, we were as comfortable around each other as if we'd grown up together. I felt like I'd known him forever.

After the show, Brad went up to LeAnn's lead guitarist and got a guitar pic for me. Later, as we were walking back to the car, we noticed a line of people waiting to go backstage. I told Brad how much I've always wanted to meet LeAnn Rimes, especially since I sang her songs on *American Idol*, and Brad began schmoozing the security guard until he finally let me go backstage to get her autograph!

I remember running into my parent's bedroom after I got home and announcing that I had just been on the best first date of my life. And the rest, as they say, is history . . .

Chapter Fourteen

Engaged!

"Ok—so I'm doing it. I'm jumping in. I'm taking the plunge. I'm getting MARRIED! Aaaah!"
—My September 9, 2005 journal entry at age 20

Pretty soon, things started getting a little more serious with Brad and I. I had never met anyone like him, but I was writing several missionaries at the time.

I wanted to wait until at least one of them got home, so I could . . . well, not compare, but . . . compare! And let me tell you, there was no comparison. Brad was it for me.

Sure, we had our typical ups and downs, and even "broke up" a time or two (and basically got back together the next day), but the more we were around each other, the more we knew we wanted to always be together. We began to talk about the possibilities of marriage. He knew I was trying to pursue a career, and accepted the fact that we would sometimes have to sacrifice in order for me to keep pursuing it.

I flew back and forth from Nashville on a monthly basis, still with no record deal in sight. I was beginning to think that maybe it would never happen for me. I had a lot of interest, but no one was willing to take the risk of signing me—except one small independent record label called Lofton Creek.

Greg and I debated over whether or not it would be smart to sign with an independent. We knew the pros and cons. We also knew that they were the only ones interested. By now, I had recorded a full CD back in Nashville, and had been pitching it all around Nashville. It had been three years since I was on *Idol* and I needed to get myself out there.

Plus, all of a sudden a young blonde girl named Carrie Underwood had come along. Everyone loved her. She ended up winning *American Idol* and had instant success. Here I was, busting my you-know-what to get a record deal, and I felt like she just had it handed to her. I couldn't listen to her songs, or look at her pictures without feeling envious.

A year later, another blonde country girl named Kellie Pickler also appeared on *Idol*. She made it all the way to the top six, just like I did, except she got signed right off the bat. Now, I was the third blonde country singer (albeit the *first*) who was trying to make it in Nashville, with still no luck. I couldn't figure out what I was doing wrong.

Faith

I went through a really dark time, right before Brad and I got engaged. I so badly wanted to marry Brad, but I didn't know if I should be focusing on launching my career instead.

Finally, one night, I got on my knees and received an undeniable conformation that it was right to keep dating Brad, and I felt peaceful about marrying him.

But my manager and family were against it. They both loved Brad, but didn't think that I should put my career on hold. They thought it would "ruin" my career if I got married.

Brad's family, on the other hand, were all for it. They told me that when I put the Lord first, everything else would fall into place. I was constantly reminded that the most important thing I could do while on this earth is get married and have a family—not be a famous country singer.

Of course, they hadn't grown up with me, and didn't know how much I'd worked for this. My family knew marriage was the most important thing, too, but thought that it could be postponed so I could follow my dreams. I didn't know where to turn.

One day my manager sat me down and said, "Okay. You need to make a choice. You can choose to either have a career, or you can get married. You can't have both." Because I was under so much pressure from everyone, I told him I'd postpone getting married.

But it was just too hard for me. Brad and I had already been dating for over a year, and there was no way we could continue to put our relationship on hold. We were at the point where we needed to break up or get married.

All of these doubts were swirling around inside my head, and I would frequently lay in bed at night just trying to figure out what would be best. Finally, one day, I decided that I would just go for it. As much as I wanted to have a career, I wanted to have a family more. I couldn't bear the thought of losing Brad. So, we decided to go for it. We were going to put our fears aside, and get married. I knew that if Brad and I had faith, things would work out.

As President Thomas S. Monson said, "We must have faith in ourselves, faith in the ability of our Heavenly Father to bless us and to guide us in our endeavors." ("A Royal Priesthood," *Ensign*, Nov 2007, 59)

Brad proposed to me on September 9, 2005. That day, we went on a hike up to the same place we went on our third date. I was sort of hoping that he'd ask me up there, but he didn't. Before we drove up, he told me this big old long story about how my ring wasn't finished yet, and they still had to ship it in from some foreign country, and blah, blah, blah—I believed it. I even went out and bought a new outfit for the day, and I can't say I wasn't a little disappointed.

As we were hiking back down the hill, Brad's best friend Kevin called.

"Hey, Carmen. You don't mind if Kevin and Lindsey come and eat with us tonight, do you?"

What could I say? Brad was taking me to a very romantic restaurant—the "Tree Room" up at Sundance. I loved Kevin and Lindsay, but I always told Brad that if he proposed to me, I wanted it done in private. Now, any hope of him actually proposing to me tonight was quickly dashed.

Disappointed, I told him that would be fine, and then we continued to hike back down the hill.

We put on clean clothes when we got to the restaurant, and as I walked in, several girls working at the front started smiling and staring at me. "Welcome," they said.

"Uh, thanks," I replied, then hurried in to the bathroom to change.

Brad and I were seated at a little corner booth in the back of the restaurant, and then suddenly, his phone rang again.

"Just a sec," he said. About ten minutes later he came back and said, "Guess what. You're not going to believe this."

"What?"

"That was Kevin—he just got a flat tire, and won't be able to come join us! Can you believe it?"

"Oh, wow! Does he need help?"

"Nah, he'll be fine. Let's eat!"

I was a little surprised at how easily Brad brushed it off, but, was secretly glad that we would get to be alone.

But Brad was acting funny. He didn't eat a lot of his meal. I actually ended up eating both our meals, I was so hungry! I couldn't understand what was wrong with him. He *always* ate a ton. Plus, he kept telling me how much he loved me. Oblivious to these subtle hints, I'd just say, "Oh, I love ya too!" and keep scarfing down the food.

After the meal, a waiter came up to us and said, "Our chef is trying out new appetizers for our menu. Would you like to try one on the house?"

Brad and I looked at each other. "What do you think?" he asked.

"Sure!"

"Great," the waiter smiled. "I'll be right back."

Several minutes later he came back, carrying a plate of what looked like clams on a bed of rock salt.

"To open, just pry them with your knife. Enjoy!"

Well, I grabbed that clam, and started going to town. It was a tight little sucker! By this time, I had spilled rock salt all over me, while Brad was just waiting patiently, holding his clam.

Finally I got it open. But there was nothing inside! I was totally confused. "What the—how do you eat these things?!" I saw a little bit of something on the inside which looked strangely like glue, and began to lick the outside of the shell.

Brad was just sitting there, letting me make a fool of myself, until I finally looked over at him to see how he was faring. "Hmm. That's weird. Let's see what's in mine!"

Slowly, Brad opened his clam shell which was lined with red

velvet on the inside, and there, sparkling back at me was the most beautiful ring I'd ever seen. I was completely in shock. I just kept saying, "Shut up. Shut up! Shut up."

Right then and there he got down on one knee and asked me to marry him. It was the absolute, perfect proposal. I was walking on air, and couldn't believe that it was actually happening. I just kept staring at my ring all night, thinking how crazy it was that in three short months, I would be the wife of the most wonderful man I'd ever met. To this day, I still feel like the luckiest woman in the world!

CHAPTER FIFTEEN

Fear is a Factor for Me!

"Imagine a world where your greatest fears become reality.' In each pulse-racing Fear Factor *episode, contestants recruited across the country battle in extreme stunts. These stunts are designed to challenge the contestants both physically and mentally."*

—Summary on TV.com/Fear Factor

A few months later, as I was busily planning the wedding, I got a crazy opportunity to be on another reality show—*Fear Factor*. I remember calling Brad and asking what I should do.

"Are you kidding me? DO IT! It'll be so awesome!"

Unfortunately, I took his advice and accepted. It was *not* "so awesome."

Now, for any of you who know anything about *Fear Factor*, it goes without saying that it's not the most "family friendly" show in the world.

A few weeks before I flew out, we were sent a contract in the mail. I was still excited at this point, and began reading through it. Close to the bottom, under the category "Women" it said:

"Two-piece bathing suit—NO EXCEPTIONS!!!"

My mom and I just sat there staring at the contract. How in the world was I going to get out of that? I had never owned nor worn a bikini, and there was no way I was going to put one on and prance around on national TV! I called my manager, Greg, who also happens to be an attorney. I begged him to call the people who worked for *Fear Factor* and ask them if there was any way I could wear a one-piece swimming suit.

Amazingly, they agreed. We actually had to add in our own paragraph in the contract, stating that I would get to choose my own wardrobe, and be under no obligation to wear a bikini.

The next week, my mom and sister and I went out shopping to find a modest swimsuit. It was much harder than I thought it would be! Finally, we found a little place in Salt Lake that had racing suits. I tried on several different ones, and decided that I'd still buy "two pieces" a one-piece suit, and some looong shorts! One suit even had the shorts already built in. I was ready for anything!

I flew out to LA in the middle of October after several weeks of strenuous workouts with a personal trainer. I have to say, that even all that training did very little to prepare me for what I was about to face.

Before our first stunt, the crew came in to give us a few pointers concerning the show's host, Joe Rogan.

"First of all, don't mention marriage, religion, or politics. Joe doesn't like talking about any of those things, and he'll win you in any argument."

Well, seeing that I was a Mormon, and engaged to the son of Utah's Lt. Governor, I knew that Joe and I wouldn't have that much in common.

I don't how it happened, but it seemed like within five minutes everyone knew I was a Mormon. I remember standing outside, waiting to do our first stunt when everyone started grilling me all at once.

"Why do you believe in abstinence before marriage? How come you can't drink coffee? Have you ever tried smoking?" and on and on and on. I answered all their questions as patiently as I could.

Later, as we were getting ready in the trailer, Tana, from *The Apprentice* came up to me and told me how much she respected me sticking up for my values. I was glad to know that at least someone was on my side.

The first stunt was a demolition derby. Basically, our job was to smash into the other cars, trying to kill their engines. The car that lasted the longest won an eight day, seven night African Safari, all inclusive to Kenya. I immediately called Brad beforehand, asking if he knew any tricks. He said, "You have to hit the front of their car, where the engine is, with the back of your car!"

Anthony Federov from Season 4 of *American Idol* was my partner in crime. The rules were, he had to drive while I shifted gears. If he grabbed the gear shift, we were eliminated. About halfway through, not even thinking, Anthony reached down.

"No!" I yelled. He immediately jerked his hand back, but it was too late. He had touched the gear shift, and there were cameras in the car to prove it.

After about 20 minutes, we heard a loud, "Carmen and Anthony! You two have won!" I was totally ecstatic, but also felt like I couldn't really accept the prize and feel good about it. Everyone was coming up to us, telling us congratulations, but Anthony and I just kept looking at each other, wondering what we should do. Finally, we both decided to tell some of the people that worked on set what had happened. They told us that they were reviewing the tapes, and not to worry.

Ten minutes later, they said, "You guys are fine. Don't worry about it. You still won the trip." Now I went crazy with excitement. We had not only won the trip, but we had been honest about our actions. I knew that I wouldn't have been able to live with myself if I had not told the truth.

The next stunt was a three-part stunt. We had to get three skulls: one from the bottom of a well, one from a stick across a mud hole, and one from inside an alligator's den. Of course, us girls were in charge of getting the skulls from the well and alligator den. But Anthony and I made it out okay, and moved on to round three.

This time, we had to ride out on the lake on a jet ski, swim to a houseboat and put out a fire, rescue a dummy from inside (80 lbs., mind you) and then hop a helicopter ride to the middle of the lake, jump out, put the dummy on a gurney, pull the dummy *and* gurney to shore, and lift it into a waiting ambulance. I have never been so physically challenged in my life.

I wore a shiny black one-piece suit this day—the one that had the shorts attached. All of the other girls were in bikinis.

As I was waiting around, one of the other contestants looked me up and down and said, "Hey, Carmen. Sexy swimming suit."

Someone stifled a laugh.

"Thanks," I replied. "You're being sarcastic, aren't you?"

He nodded. "You're a sexy chick. Why don't you show it off?"

I shrugged and said, "I'm saving that for my husband." Silence. Nobody had anything to say after that.

Again, Anthony and I made it through another round, and the next stunt included being lowered into the water in a water-proof air-tight box with madagascar beetles, roaches and maggots. Not fun.

But by far, the worst stunt on that show was being tied down at the waist and cuffed at the hands and feet on a rickety old sled. Anthony had to find three keys that were in cans in a huge ice chest in order to wheel the sled down a tiny tunnel, where I had to get three keys with my mouth. At each of the three places, I would get loads of TARANTULAS *dumped* directly on my face. IT WAS HORRIBLE!!!

I have never, ever been so afraid of anything in my life. My whole body was shaking as Anthony first wheeled me down the tunnel. We did pretty good at first, but unfortunately Anthony never found the last can with the key inside to wheel me back, and I was stuck at the end of the tunnel with the spiders for TWENTY THREE MINUTES!!!

I could feel the tarantulas biting me as I waited in a panic for Anthony to wheel me back. I was in a sort of trance as I was pulled from the sled, and had been closing my mouth so tightly so as to not get any spiders in my *mouth* as I tried to get the keys with my tongue and teeth, that my lips were swollen, and I actually damaged a nerve. But that wasn't even the worst part! We learned the hard way that when tarantulas get nervous, they inject tiny little hairs into your body as a defense mechanism that feel like little splinters or pieces of fiberglass stuck all over your body.

We were told that duct tape helped pull out the hairs, and us girls spent the evening sticking it on and ripping it off. It took over *two weeks* for those sharp little hairs to come out, and was the most painful thing I've ever been through!

Anthony and I made it all the way to the last stunt. All we had to do was stand on cars 100 feet in the air while one of us threw balls to the other person as the cars moved apart. After 60 seconds, we were ejected from the cars, they crashed together and blew up, and whatever team caught the most balls won. We only caught two balls, and finished in second place.

But at that point, I honestly didn't care that much. It had been ten days since I'd last seen my fiance, and I wanted to get off of that show as fast as I could.

While I was on the *Fear Factor*, I had the opportunity to give one of the *Survivor* contestants a copy of the Book of Mormon. We had an awesome discussion one day about the Church, and luckily I had brought a cheap $3.00 book with me that I used to travel with.

A few months later, she called and said that the missionaries had been to her house, and were teaching her. I don't know if anything ever came of it, but a tiny seed had been planted. I was so happy that even in a such an awful situation, I was given the opportunity to share the gospel with someone.

CHAPTER SIXTEEN

Hakuna Matata

"Did the airlines lose your luggage?"
—An American woman whose luggage
was also lost on the way to Africa

Well, before I knew it, the spider hairs had all worked their way out and the big day of the wedding had arrived! I went through the Bountiful Temple five days before my wedding to receive my endowments, and it was the most beautiful thing I'd ever experienced. I was glowing.

Three days before I got married, I flew out to Nashville to do a showcase for Capitol records. I was so nervous to go out of town so soon before the wedding, but all went well and I made it back okay.

The day before we were married, as I was saying goodbye to everyone that came to our wedding dinner, I had an overwhelming feeling of peace come over me. I had never felt so happy or peaceful. It wasn't the jump for joy, scream and shout jittery happiness I felt when I was chosen to be in the Top 12 of *American Idol*. It was an overwhelming, quiet peace that filled every cell of my body.

On December 15, 2005 I was sealed to my sweetheart for time and all eternity in the Bountiful, Utah temple. The entire day was bliss. Even when I forgot my veil and my mom had to run home and grab it while the wedding party stood freezing outside, I was happy. Nothing in the world has compared to the joy I've felt being Brad's wife. I knew I loved him that day but since then my love has grown so much deeper, and stronger, and truer. Every day I wake up and think how lucky I am to be his wife.

One day as we were driving home from a family vacation to California, my father-in-law turned around from the driver's seat and said, "Hey. Do you realize that if Carmen wasn't on *American Idol*, you two never would have met?"

That startled me. Because I had been on that show, I had been asked to perform at the Stadium of Fire, where Brad and I met. Because he lived in Orem, and I in Bountiful, the chances of ever running into each other were slim to none. We sat in silence, just thinking about how our lives had been guided by the hand of the Lord.

Good Works

A few months before our one-year anniversary, Brad and I were able to take that trip I had won on *Fear Factor*, and we headed to Kenya, Africa for one of the biggest adventures of our lives.

We flew from Salt Lake to Chicago to London to Nairobi. The flights were extremely long, and after traveling for two days, Brad and I couldn't wait to change into some fresh clothes and take a shower. As soon as we landed in Nairobi, we went through customs then downstairs to the baggage claim area. We watched all sorts of bags go around and around the carousel, but didn't see ours. I started to panic, and Brad told me not to freak out just yet—after all, someone's bags had to be last! After about fifteen minutes, the carousel stopped, and there was no sign of either of our bags. I assumed it was now time to begin freaking out and sat there crying by the carousel while Brad went to find someone who could help us.

Turns out, our bags were still in the U.S., and we were promised that they were going to be sending them tomorrow.

Brad and I mostly slept that day, and the next morning awoke to find a wonderful variety of fresh-squeezed mango, orange, grapefruit, and other juices along with omelets, waffles, fresh syrup, pastries, fruit, and many other delicious things to eat downstairs. Africa was beautiful. I had never seen so many different varieties of animals and plant life.

We were in the city the first day, and then out in the mountains near Mount Kenya for day two. We still had no luggage, and every time we'd ask our tour guides if they knew anything about where our bags were, they'd just say, "Hakuna matata—no worries!"

I got really sick of hearing that phrase. I couldn't help but worry! Not only were we stuck wearing the same dirty clothes we'd had on for the past three days, but Brad had left his medication in his checked luggage, so he had not been able to take his malaria pills. We prayed and prayed that somehow, far away in the mountains of Africa, our bags would find us.

We stayed at a neat place called The Ark for day two. It had a huge watering hole in front, and every hour when a new animal was sighted, a little bell would ring in our rooms so we could walk out and see it. We saw a momma and baby elephant, a buffalo, some antelope, and all different kinds of birds. That night, as we were talking to some ladies from California about our luggage being lost, they suddenly insisted I take some of their clothes, toiletries, and insect repellent. One lady even had the exact same medication as Brad, and gave him a few pills to take for the next few days.

We were so grateful and overwhelmed at their generosity. Not only did they give me clothes to wear, but they were some of their *nicest* clothes. They freely gave me a Gap cashmere sweater, Juicy velour pants, soft long-sleeved cotton shirts, and so many other things that were way too nice. But they didn't even blink at the gifts. They sort of took Brad and I under their wings. I was so touched at their generosity, that that night I prayed and told Heavenly Father that when and if my luggage ever arrived, I'd also look for someone who was in need and give of my substance as well.

The day before we left on a plane to go out to the Masai Mara, Brad's bag arrived. My bag was delivered to the tiny airport in Nairobi just ten minutes before our flight took off for day five of our trip.

We landed on a dirt runway out in the middle of nowhere. This is where the real African safari began. On our first game drive, we saw elephants, giraffes, buffalo, wildebeests, and all sorts of other animals. It was incredible. I felt like I had stepped into *The Lion King* movie.

To say I was nervous about being out in the wild with lions and leopards and elephants is a serious understatement. Nighttime in Africa is especially creepy. There is an animal called the tree hyrax that comes out when the sun goes down and makes a noise that sounds like someone is screaming in pain. I kept hearing little things brush up against our tent all night long, and we even found a lizard on the wall!

I felt much better when the sun came up. On the last day of our trip, we went down to the Safari Club to eat breakfast. Brad got up to get some food, and as I was waiting at the table, I saw a pretty blonde girl sitting next to me that was about my age. We began talking, and she told me she was on her honeymoon. All of a sudden, out of the blue, she said, "Did the airlines lose your luggage?" Surprised, I told her they had, and asked if they lost hers, too.

"Yes," she replied. "My husband and I don't have anything!"

Soon Brad came back, carrying a plate of food. I told him what had happened, and after breakfast, we went back to our tent to see what we could give them. I put together a little kit of things similar to what the ladies from California gave me. I didn't have any Juicy pants or cashmere sweaters to give her, but I did pack some extra shirts and socks and pajamas and bug spray. Now that we had our luggage and were returning home the next day, we figured we could give up some of the things we didn't need.

It felt so good to walk up to her tent and hand her the little bag. She was so grateful, and so was I to all of those sweet ladies from California for setting such a good example for me.

Playing on stage at the Stadium of Fire.

It was during this performance that Brad said he fell in love with me.

Our third date on a hike up to Stewart Falls near Sundance, Utah. This was the day I fell in love with Brad.

In ribbons and curls with my older sister Camille, on the left, and cousin Heidi at a bridal shower thrown for me.

Brad and I on our wedding day, December 15th, 2005.

CHAPTER SEVENTEEN

And the Beat Goes On...

"You have a deep, deep passion for music. I see it when you sing—you sing from your heart."
—My husband Brad, February 15, 2007

I've often wondered why I made it onto *American Idol*. Certainly, there were others that were better than me. I didn't have to get called back to be on the Wildcard show. But one of the reasons I think I was "meant to do this" as my mom always said, was so I could be guided to my future husband. So many wonderful opportunities have come my way because of that show. My life didn't exactly work out the way I had planned it—but there definitely has been a plan.

I can honestly say that the day I went through the temple, I was changed. I felt like my life had taken a beautiful turn for the better. I felt that no matter what happened, I was doing what was right. I could've postponed my marriage. I could have moved to Nashville and prayed that things would work out in the end with Brad. I could've moved out to L.A. to pursue acting. But I chose to put my marriage first, and it was the best decision I've ever made.

In January of 2007 I finally signed on with Lofton Creek Records. I went on a radio promotion tour at the beginning of 2007. I was gone five days a week for about 12 weeks on my very own tour bus, promoting my single "Nothin' Like the Summer," a song I co-wrote with Victoria Shaw and Jason Deere. It was tough leaving Brad. I didn't like being away from him.

Before I left for my promotion tour, my husband knelt down beside me and said, "You need to do this for three reasons. First, because you can be a great example to the world. Second, because you have a deep, deep passion for music. I see it when you sing—you sing from your heart. And third, to be financially free. When times get tough out there, you need to remember why you're doing this."

A lot people have asked me why in the world I would choose to get married at the young age of 20. I was told that because I chose to get married, I'd lose a lot of my male fan base. I was told that people wouldn't take me seriously. I was told that my career would be ruined. To all of that, I can only say that no matter what happens in the future, the decision I made to get married was right for me.

Most people don't look at marriage the way we do. It is a lifelong commitment—more than that—it is an *eternal* commitment! *The most important commitment!* I see that as the greatest blessing I could ever have. To know that if I live faithfully I get to be with my husband forever is the greatest "achievement" I could ever ask for.

There is nothing that is more important than marrying the "right person, at the right place, at the right time." DO NOT let ANYTHING or ANYONE stand in your way of achieving that goal. I decided that I was willing to sacrifice my career, if necessary, to have a family. While it hasn't been easy, I know it was the right decision, and I don't regret it for a minute.

I've often wondered where my life will lead me. I haven't sold a million CDs. I haven't had a Billboard number one hit. I haven't been nominated for a Grammy. I may never achieve any of those things.

However, I've tried my hardest to develop faith, remember who I am and know that I have infinite worth and that I am literally a daughter of God with a divine nature. I've strived to live my life with integrity and I continually try to do good works. I understand that I have the free agency to choose who I will become. I have a great desire to let the Spirit guide me and direct my life. The Young Women values and standards of the church have helped me immeasurably, and I'm excited for what the future holds!

I'm still going around, trying to pursue my country music career. I released an album at the end of August. I've been performing all around the country with my band. I love the feeling of being up on stage, doing what I love.

It's still a challenge for me to musically "stay in tune." In fact, it's one of my greatest weaknesses. I have to practice every day to train my voice to hit the notes at the right pitches. Even if I'm just slightly "off" it's very noticeable. Even people with no musical capability can tell when something doesn't sound quite right. Growing up, whenever our piano was out of tune we had it fixed right away. The longer we waited, the worse it became. The mechanic used a tuning fork to perfectly tune the strings back to the right pitches. He tightened or loosened them, depending on what needed to be done. Singing is similar. I need to make my vocal chords get either thicker or thinner, depending on what notes I need to hit. It's a lot of hard work to make sure that I'm always on tune when I sing. I know I won't be perfect all the time, but the harder I work at it, the better I get.

Staying in tune spiritually can also be a challenge for me. I have to pay attention to the little things in life. Even if I'm doing something that is just slightly off the straight and narrow path, I notice a big difference in my life. I feel unsettled when I leave mistakes unresolved, and usually the longer I wait to correct them, the harder it is to get back on track.

But when I do what's right and my life is in harmony with the gospel, I feel happy and am at peace. I've noticed that even people who are not of our faith can see a difference in the way Latter-day Saint men and women live their lives. I may not always be perfect. In fact, I'll probably need a good "tuning" now and again.

But the Savior can be *my* "tuning fork." He is a perfect example, the one I try to pattern my life after. I know that if I "listen" carefully to Him, He will always keep me "in tune"!

Also by
Carmen Rasmusen

Don't miss Carmen's first full-length CD, *Nothin' Like the Summer*. Produced by Lofton Creek Records, this nationally released CD has gained strong reviews and is filled with upbeat country songs such as "Happy," "Love Will Wait," and "Shine," as well as the hit title track.

It is available through Wal-Mart and other major retailers, and is sold online at Amazon.com and Loftoncreek.com.

Carmen enjoys giving stake firesides and musical performances. Contact her at **carmen@springcreekbooks.com** to schedule an event in your area.